HUGGING

THE

UNCERTAINTY

TAKE CARE OF MOM

IN ITS

JOURNEY WITH DEMENTIA

Almangie Ruefli

Dedication

To my dear mother, whose love and courage in her journey with dementia have been my greatest inspiration. Who somehow contributed to the care of my mother, and to my beloved daughter Angie, always by my side with unconditional love and support. To all the brave caregivers facing daily challenges with unwavering love. May these pages offer comfort, understanding, and hope on your journey.

Acknowledgment

I would like to express my profound gratitude to all the people who have been a fundamental part of creating this book. First and foremost, to my beloved mother, whose courageous journey with dementia inspired every word on these pages. Her strength and love have left an indelible mark on my heart.

I appreciate my siblings for the support they have somehow provided me during this challenging process, and to my husband for his cooperation and patience.

Special thanks to my daughter Angie, whose presence has been my anchor in emotional storms. Your unconditional love and support have been my greatest strength.

I also want to acknowledge caregivers and healthcare professionals who face dementia with dedication and compassion every day. Their shared experiences have enriched these pages and offer hope to those walking similar paths.

Thanks to my friends and all those who have shared their stories, advice, and words of encouragement. Their generosity has shaped this project and created an invaluable support network.

Finally, I appreciate the editorial team for their professionalism and commitment. Thank you for believing in this story and helping bring it to a wider audience.

This book is a tribute to resilience, love, and community. To all of you, my heartfelt thanks.

Table Of Contents

Introduction

In the journey of life, we often encounter unexpected paths and unfathomable challenges. When dementia knocks on our doors, we face a journey filled with uncertainty and profound changes. In this voyage, we become caregivers, life companions to those who now confront an ocean of forgetfulness and confusion.

The purpose of this book is to share tools of assistance and caregiver experiences from those, like you and me, who daily live the intense struggle of caring for loved ones affected by dementia. Within these pages, you will find authentic stories, practical advice, and a space where the caregiver community comes together to share knowledge and support. This book is a beacon of understanding and guidance, designed to illuminate your path amid the challenges presented by dementia. Together, we will explore paths, learn from each other, and find solace in the community formed on this journey.

Embracing Uncertainty: Caring for Mom on Her Journey with Dementia

Inspiring Stories and Tips for Caregivers invite you to explore this journey with us. Through touching narratives, shared experiences, and valuable advice, you will discover that in the midst of uncertainty, there is an unyielding strength that emanates from love and dedication. These pages are woven with stories of caregivers who, like you, confront dementia with courage and compassion.

We will guide you through this journey, sharing knowledge, strategies, and emotional support so that you face each challenge with confidence and love. Because in uncertainty, we find the opportunity to discover deeper love, family unity, and the power of compassion.

Join us as we explore the complexities of caring for those we love on their journey with dementia. Through commitment and community, we will learn that even in the darkness of uncertainty, we can find the light of unbreakable love.

Almangie Ruefli

Chapter 1

Dementia, the Tapestry of Fading Memories

ALMANGIE RUEFLI

"When the Threads of Memory Begin to Fade"

It was a transformation that wove itself slowly, like the golden leaves of autumn falling one by one. The loss of short-term memory, seemingly harmless at first, became the guiding thread that led us down an unexpected path. We recall the initial signs as fragments of a story in the making, a tale being written with the fading memories of my mother as its ink.

With a touch of resignation in our smiles, we thought that everyone forgets small things. Forgetting where we left the keys, the name of an old friend, or the date of a medical appointment was not uncommon. But like a clock marking the inexorable passage of time, we began to notice that the gaps in my mother's memory became more frequent and prominent.

My mother, the passionate cook of a small elderly residence who delighted generations with her homemade flavors and the love she infused into every dish, began to set aside certain recipes. The kindness and compassion she had poured into her work were no longer as evident. The notes she left on how to perfect her morning coffee became confusing, as if the words resisted staying on paper.

The signs, subtle at first, began to accumulate. Names that used to flow naturally in conversations were now avoided, as if hiding in an unreachable corner of her mind. Moments that she once celebrated with joy were recorded in a notebook, as an attempt to retain what was fading away.

It was then that the impact of this transformation became deeper, more distressing. Explanations fit together like pieces of a puzzle but failed to complete the picture entirely. The diagnosis of coronavirus, a disease that left traces on the memories of the elderly, seemed the obvious answer. We thought my mother would recover, as if the strength of her spirit could sweep away the clouds of confusion surrounding her.

The backdrop of our optimism was interwoven with the fibers of hope and fear. Hope that the skills that seemed to fade would return, that the woman who had faced life with determination and love would emerge once more. Fear that this transformation was not temporary, that what we were facing was the beginning of an unpredictable and challenging journey.

As we explore the pages of this chapter, we invite readers to travel the path that led us to recognize the early signs of dementia. We delve into the vulnerability of uncertainty and attempts to rationalize the inexplicable. This is the beginning of a shared journey, where fading memories become a tapestry revealing the depth of the human experience in all its beauty and fragility.

In the following pages, we will explore how we face the unknown, how we seek answers, and how we learn to support each other as the tapestry continues its unpredictable weaving.

Chapter 2

Symptoms Painting a Changing Reality

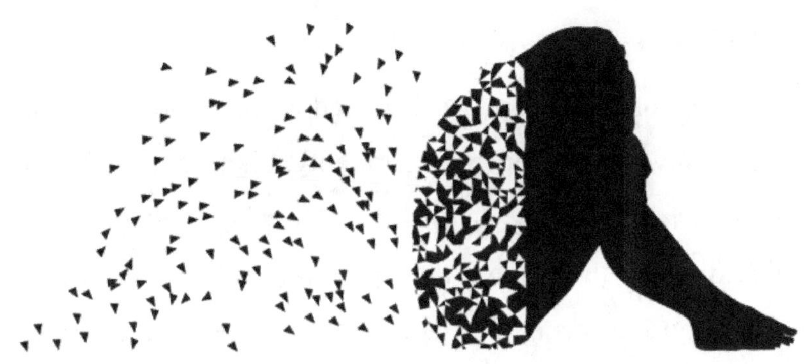

"When the Threads of Memory Slip Through the Fingers"

As the clock of time advanced, her mind wove a tapestry of fading memories that knew no boundaries. Symptoms presented themselves like strokes of a constantly changing painting, portraying a shifting reality that left us heartbroken and strengthened in determination.

Memory loss, once considered a common and ordinary puzzle, evolved into a much darker reality. Like leaves falling in the autumn wind, names, dates, and everyday details gradually vanished. And though each chapter faded, new shadows also appeared on the scene. Her faded face, apathy towards irrelevant events, showed signs of depression.

The relationship between **Alzheimer's and depression** exists and is often complex. It can sometimes create confusion in diagnosis, but the symptoms of both diseases can coexist. This can happen as a consequence of pathological brain alterations or as a reactive depressive mood to the knowledge of the Alzheimer's diagnosis and its consequences.

It is important to **inform the specialist of possible depressive** signs in the affected person so that appropriate treatment measures can be taken and to follow advice aimed at **alleviating their sorrow.**

Our hearts broke

Seeing her struggle with what she once effortlessly mastered. Appliances, once reliable friends, became a maze of confusion for her. The clothes dryer and microwave, objects that occupied a place in her everyday world, intertwined in her mind, forming a knot that ceased to be unraveled.

The spectacle of watching her try to dry clothes in the microwave was etched in our memory, a mix of surprise and sadness. The incidents that unfolded revealed cracks in the bridge between the past and the present, between familiarity and confusion.

The weight of reality united us as siblings on a shared mission: to face this giant before us, a reality that challenged notions of normalcy. Concern intertwined with determination as we confronted the looming storm.

To understand this metamorphosis, we turned to those who could shed light on the growing darkness. The doctor, a silent witness to the progression of dementia in other patients, extended a hand of empathy and knowledge. He explained how dementia, in its multiple forms, can affect brain functions and memories, turning everyday moments into a constantly changing puzzle.

Concern for the symptoms we had observed was confirmed. Difficulty performing tasks that were once natural, confusion with everyday objects, and memory loss were common characteristics in the progression of dementia and Alzheimer's. The puzzle pieces began to fit, forming an image we had feared but needed to face.

And so, with knowledge in our hands and determination in our hearts, we began to join forces to support my mother in her fight against the tide of forgetfulness. We faced a changing reality with the hope of providing stability and love in a world fading before her eyes.

In the pages that follow, we will explore how we faced these symptoms that outlined a landscape in constant transformation. We will delve into the challenges of adapting to a new normal and the search for ways to maintain love and connection as reality slips through our fingers.

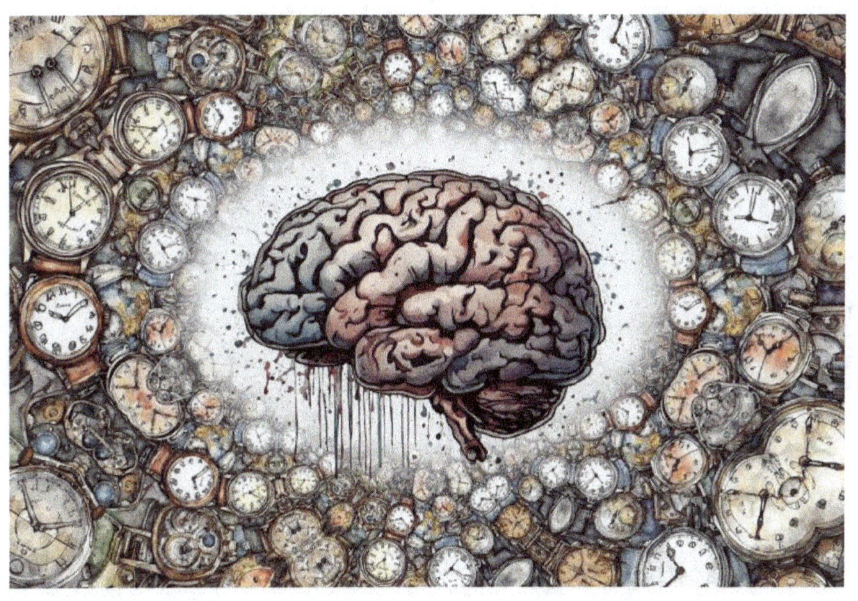

Chapter 3

Between Shadows and Certainties: The Diagnosis of Dementia

"Opening Eyes to the Truth"

The dark days of uncertainty led us to a crossroads: how could we accurately understand the metamorphosis occurring in our mother's mind? As we grappled with the confusion of fading symptoms and traces of memory, the time came to seek answers beyond our assumptions and fears.

Unmistakable Signs: *Recognizing the Need for Diagnosis*

Symptoms, like puzzle pieces coming together more clearly as we progressed, led us to the conclusion that the situation went beyond what we could attribute to age or even the aftermath of the coronavirus. Confusion with everyday objects, gaps in memory, and difficulty in performing basic tasks became unmistakable shadows that needed to be explored further.

"Everyone makes mistakes, but people with dementia may increasingly struggle to perform tasks such as handling monthly bills or following a cooking recipe, as noted by the Alzheimer's Association. They may also face difficulties concentrating on tasks, experience a prolongation in the time needed to carry them out, or have trouble completing them.

Asking the same question over and over or repeating the same story about a recent event several times are common indicators of mild or moderate Alzheimer's disease, according to the Cleveland Clinic.

Not feeling particularly sociable from time to time is one thing, but a sudden and routine loss of interest in family, friends, work, and social events is a warning sign of dementia. A new study published in the *Journal of Alzheimer's* Disease found that apathy can even be a sign that someone is progressing from mild cognitive impairment (MCI) — symptoms of memory loss or thinking problems not as severe as dementia — to Alzheimer's disease. Those with MCI have a higher risk of developing dementia."

The Value of Communication: *Opening the Door to Medical Dialogue*

Our first line of defense was to open a dialogue with the doctor. Seated in the waiting room, my sister, my mother, and I, our minds and hearts were filled with questions and a mix of hope and fear. How is a diagnosis made? What tests could reveal the truth behind the shadows? The doctor greeted us with empathy, knowing that we were seeking answers that could provide us with a path forward, and she spoke to us about the different tests and tools that could aid in an accurate diagnosis.

The Art of Assessment: *Diagnostic Tests and Tools*

The process of diagnosing dementia is a combination of art and science. It is based on a comprehensive assessment that spans from medical history to cognitive tests and laboratory analysis. Cognitive tests, such as the Mini-Mental State Examination (MMSE) or the Montreal Cognitive Assessment (MoCA), evaluate memory, abstract thinking, and other key cognitive functions.

To diagnose the cause of dementia, the healthcare professional must recognize the pattern of loss of skills and functions. The doctor also determines what the person is still capable of doing. Recently, biomarkers have been used to make a more precise diagnosis of Alzheimer's disease.

A healthcare professional reviews your medical history and symptoms, conducts a physical examination, and may ask someone close about your symptoms.

There is no single test for diagnosing dementia. Doctors are likely to perform a series of tests that can help pinpoint the problem.

Cognitive and neuropsychological tests

In these tests, your thinking ability is assessed. A series of tests measure thinking skills, such as memory, orientation, reasoning and judgment, language skills, and attention.

Neurological evaluation

Memory, language skills, visual perception, attention, problem-solving ability, movement, senses, balance, reflexes, and other areas are evaluated.

Brain scans

• **Computed tomography or magnetic resonance imaging.** These scans can check for evidence of stroke, bleeding, tumor, or fluid accumulation, known as hydrocephalus.

• **Positron emission tomography scans.** In these scans, brain activity patterns can be observed. They help determine if there are deposits of the protein amyloid, also called tau, in the brain, which is a characteristic hallmark of Alzheimer's disease.

Laboratory analysis

Simple blood tests can detect physical problems that may affect brain function, such as a lack of vitamin B-12 in the body or an underactive thyroid gland. Occasionally, cerebrospinal fluid is analyzed to check for the presence of infection, inflammation, or markers of some degenerative diseases.

Psychiatric evaluation

A mental health professional can determine if depression or another mental health condition contributes to the symptoms.

(Dementia mayoclinic.org)

Exploring the Brain

Imaging Tests. Magnetic resonance imaging (MRI) and positron emission tomography (PET) are tools that allow doctors to explore the brain for structural changes and accumulation of abnormal proteins, such as beta-amyloid plaques associated with Alzheimer's. These tests provide a window into brain physiology that complements clinical information.

The Diagnosis: *More than a Label, a Guide*

Once the results of evaluations and tests are obtained, the diagnosis takes shape. It is not just a label but a guide that helps us understand the nature of the transformation happening in the brain. The diagnosis gives us a compass to navigate the unknown terrain, make informed decisions, and find ways to maintain love and support.

For Sally, accepting her husband's diagnosis was not easy. Alfie, my husband, worked as a foreman in one of the gold mines in South Africa, "Sally explains." When he told me he wanted to retire, I was stunned. He was only 56 and a very intelligent and hardworking man. His coworkers later told me that he was making strange judgment errors, and they had often covered for him.

"When he retired, we bought a hotel. Since Alfie was handy, I thought he would take care of the building maintenance. However, he always called someone else to make repairs."

That same year, we went on vacation to Durban beach with our three-year-old granddaughter. She loved playing on a trampoline across the street, right in front of the apartment where we stayed. One afternoon, around four-thirty, Alfie took her to jump on the trampoline and said they would be back in half an hour. Seven o'clock came, and they still hadn't returned. I called the police, but they explained that they couldn't initiate a search for a person until at least twenty-four hours had passed missing. That night, I thought I was going crazy, imagining that they had been killed. The next day, around noon, they knocked on the door, and when I opened it, there was Alfie with the girl in his arms."

"—Where did you go?" I asked.

"—Don't be mad at me," he replied. "I don't know."

"—Grandma," clarified the little girl, "we got lost."

"Imagine that. Getting lost across the street! I still don't know where they slept that night. Well, at least a friend of mine found them and showed them which was our apartment."

After this incident, Sally took Alfie to a neurologist, who diagnosed him with dementia (loss of mental functions). It turned out that Alfie had Alzheimer's disease, for which there is still no effective treatment or cure. The British magazine New Scientist says that Alzheimer's "ranks fourth among the most lethal diseases in the developed world, after heart disease, cancer, and stroke." It has been called "the leading chronic disease of old age," although it can also appear at a relatively young age, as was the case with Alfie.

With the progressively increasing life expectancy in prosperous countries, the forecasts regarding the number of people suffering from dementia are alarming. A study pointed out that the percentage increase between 1980 and 2000 could be 14% in Britain, 33% in the United States, and 64% in Canada. An Australian television documentary presented in 1990 said, "It is estimated that there are currently 100,000 people with Alzheimer's in Australia. By the end of the century, the figure will be 200,000." It is estimated that by the year 2023, there will be over 100 million Alzheimer's patients worldwide.

[Notes] Alzheimer's disease is named after Alois Alzheimer, a German neurologist who first described it in 1906 after performing an autopsy on a patient who had died in a severe state of dementia. Alzheimer's is estimated to constitute 60% of all dementias and affects 1 in 10 people over the age of 65. There is a particular type of dementia, called multi-infarct dementia, which occurs as a result of a series of mild strokes that damage the brain.

Warning: Before concluding that a person has Alzheimer's, it is essential to undergo a thorough medical examination. Between ten and twenty percent of dementia cases originate from treatable conditions. Regarding the diagnosis of Alzheimer's, the book "How to Care for Aging Parents" explains: "Alzheimer's can only be diagnosed with certainty by studying the brain during an autopsy, but doctors can rule out other possibilities and arrive at the diagnosis through the process of elimination."

As we progress in this chapter, we delve into the search for answers and the confrontation of the truth revealed by the medical evaluation. We explore how the diagnosis, though difficult to receive, provided us with a deeper understanding of the journey we faced. With the diagnosis in hand, we learned to weave a new perspective and find ways to embrace reality with love and strength.

Chapter 4

The Diagnosis: Crucial Decisions in the Family

"Between Crossroads and Unbreakable Unity"

The diagnosis, like a compass showing us the way through unknown terrain, not only brings the truth of dementia but also a series of decisions branching out like paths in all directions. In this chapter, we will explore how we faced these crucial decisions as a family, navigating through the challenges and opportunities that lay before us.

Emotions on the Surface: *Acceptance and Resistance*

The news of emotions did not come without its wave of tumultuous feelings. From acceptance to resistance, our family experienced a storm of emotions. Acceptance provided the necessary clarity to address the decisions ahead. Resistance, though natural, became a reminder of how deep our love and concern were woven.

The diagnosis of dementia shook the foundations of our family in ways we could never have anticipated. Acceptance and resistance intertwined in a whirlwind of emotions that challenged our notions of our mother and ourselves.

Denial as a Protective Shield

The news hit us like a blast of icy wind, a reality that seemed inconceivable. It wasn't easy to accept that the strong and independent woman we had known all our lives was undergoing such a profound transformation. Denial became a protective shield, a way to preserve the image of our mother as we had known her.

When a family member is diagnosed with dementia, denial is a common reaction among relatives. It can be overwhelming to accept the reality of the disease and its implications. Some reasons for denial include fear of the unknown, hope that symptoms will disappear, fear of the emotional and physical burden of care, and difficulty accepting the progressive loss of the loved one's capabilities.

It is important to recognize that denial is part of the emotional process, and each person experiences it uniquely. Family members may need time to assimilate the news and adapt to the new reality. Open communication, emotional support, and information about dementia can aid in the acceptance process.

The Importance of Understanding Our Own Emotions and Feelings

At the same time, it is crucial to understand ourselves as family members and caregivers. It is important to identify our own feelings and emotions: how we reacted upon receiving the diagnosis, how we have evolved emotionally since then, or how we fit and interpret the way our loved one behaves.

Each person processes the news and reacts to the diagnosis

differently. Personal characteristics, sensitivity, and personality are factors that influence this.

After the news, a torrent of emotions and sensations is unleashed, initiating the journey toward accepting the disease. In reality, it is a grieving process, during which different phases are traversed. These often overlap or fluctuate throughout the disease.

The Internal Struggle with Vulnerability

Our mother, a woman who always stood with determination and courage, now stood at a crossroads. Dementia had taken away the tools she had always used to fight her battles. Tears that were rarely shed before now moistened her eyes, revealing the vulnerability that had been hidden beneath layers of strength.

From our childhood, we never saw our mother cry in the face of the adversities she encountered. She fought tirelessly to raise her five children, resisting even in the most difficult situations. Her strength, independence, and capability were defining traits.

Life had shaped her over the years, turning her into a strong woman.

Seeing her so vulnerable to dementia is an overwhelming challenge for us. Watching her struggle against something that has no clear sense, resisting depending on our help, and trying to handle things her way adds an additional layer of complexity to this battle.

Despite my attempts to explain what is happening, I have not succeeded. I have tried to help her accept her vulnerability and allow herself to flow, but my efforts have been in vain. Perhaps the key is that I myself need to accept the situation in her way, adapt to her pace, and understand her unique way of acceptance.

The Challenge of Adaptation

Before us was a different woman, one who often seemed lost in her own world. Decisions that she once made with certainty became overwhelming dilemmas. Indecision and fear seized her face, marking a contrast with the image of the woman who always knew where she was going and how to get there.

The challenge of adaptation for a person with dementia lies in confronting the progressive loss of cognitive and functional abilities. As the disease advances, the ability to perform everyday tasks, remember information, and engage in conversation decreases. Adapting to these limitations can lead to frustration, confusion, and anxiety in the affected person. Additionally, dementia can alter the perception of the environment, making it even more difficult to adapt to new situations or changes in routine. Compassionate and personalized support is essential to help the person face these challenges and maintain the quality of life as much as possible.

The Struggle for Identity

Seeing our mother wrestle with her identity was an emotional blow. The woman who was once a beacon of strength now struggled to recognize herself in the mirror. Each moment of forgetfulness or confusion seemed to erase a part of who she was. We faced the painful truth that we were losing not only the mother we knew but also the woman she had been.

This challenge can generate distress and anxiety as the person confronts the loss of connection with their own history and personality.

Dementia affects memory and cognitive functions, contributing to the struggle of identity. Caregivers and family members play a crucial role in providing emotional support, recalling events, and sharing memories to help maintain a connection with the person's past identity. As the disease progresses, adapting to this new reality and embracing the changing identity becomes a delicate but important process.

Resistance to Letting Go of Hope

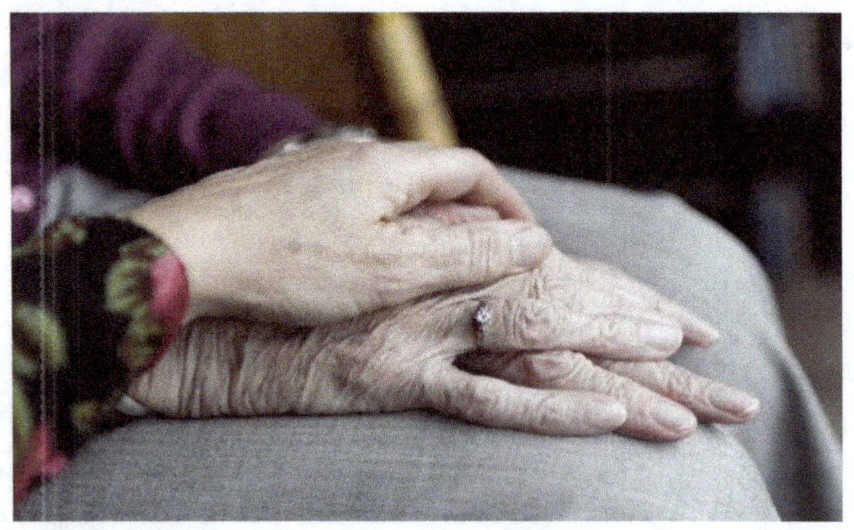

Resistance, although natural, was also a constant on our journey. We clung to the hope that, somehow, she would regain her former identity. We resisted the idea that this transformation could be permanent. Despite the harsh reality before us, the desire to see her strong and determined again lingered in our hearts.

Resistance to letting go of hope is a common struggle among families facing dementia. Hope is often associated with the possibility of the person's condition improving or stabilizing. However, dementia is a progressive disease with no known cure, leading to an emotional battle in accepting this reality.

Families may hold on to hope for innovative treatments, miraculous medications, or the belief that the situation will improve on its own. This resistance may stem from the difficulty of accepting the gradual loss of their loved one's identity and abilities. Accepting the irreversible nature of dementia involves a process of grief and adaptation.

Overcoming resistance requires a delicate balance between maintaining hope in aspects that can still be controlled, such as improving the quality of life and finding ways for emotional connection, while realistically addressing the course of the disease. Emotional support and education about dementia are crucial to help families navigate this challenging process.

Decisions that Forge New Paths

Resistance sometimes led us to difficult but necessary decisions. Deciding who would care for her and attend to her needs was a responsibility that weighed on our shoulders. Each choice forged a new path in this unknown journey. Discussions were filled with emotions and concerns but also infused with love and determination to do what was best for her.

Family decisions play a crucial role in forging new paths when facing dementia. These decisions encompass diverse aspects, from care planning to emotional coping strategies. Some key areas include:

Care Planning

Deciding on the type of care to be provided, whether at home with the help of external caregivers or considering specialized facilities such as nursing homes or dementia care centers.

Long-term care can be provided either at home or elsewhere. At some point, the person with dementia may require full-time assistance or may exhibit behaviors, such as aggression and wandering, that make home unsafe. People needing full-time help can move to a residential care facility, nursing home, or assisted living facility that can provide many or all of the long-term care services they need. When planning this care, it might be helpful to think about:

- *Where the person will live as they age and how their residence can best support their safety and meet their needs.*

- *What services are available in the community and how much they cost.*

- *How far in advance you need to plan so the person can make important decisions while they still have the capacity to do so.*

(For more information and resources, visit Alzheimer's Association)

Roles and Responsibilitie

"Distributing roles and responsibilities among family members involves establishing clear communication about who will take on various tasks related to care and decision-making."

In dementia care, the need for assistance begins long before the dementia fully presents itself. A patient with mild cognitive impairment (MCI) or in the early stages of dementia, although capable of making decisions, may still need help organizing schedules, managing finances, and maintaining a social calendar. A close relative, often a spouse or adult child, can offer assistance, often unaware that this is the beginning of a caregiving relationship. Some caregivers work as a team: a mother and daughter helping a father, or siblings working together to assist a mother. However, in most cases, there is a single caregiver who takes on the majority of caregiving responsibilities.

As dementia progresses, the patient's needs become more personal and time-consuming. Dementia often causes changes in personality and communication skills that caregivers find distressing. Physical and emotional needs become more demanding, and a caregiver will need to use the assistance of external resources, such as family members, friends, professional caregivers, and community organizations.

While a family caregiver may manage full assistance in the early stages of dementia, in later stages, it becomes impossible to provide care alone without the potential for serious safety risks for both the patient and the caregiver. Identifying exactly when caregiving responsibilities become too demanding is one of the most significant challenges for caregivers of dementia patients.

Dementia usually progresses gradually, in small increments, over several years. So do caregiving tasks. Given the incremental nature of dementia care, a caregiver may not recognize the point where the burden becomes too much and exceeds safety levels. Therefore, it is essential to delegate responsibilities to others in the family.

Education and Awareness

"Deciding to seek information and education about dementia is crucial. Understanding the disease is fundamental to making informed decisions and providing the best possible care."

Emotional Support

Deciding how to provide and receive emotional support within the family is essential. Recognizing the importance of sharing emotions, seeking professional help if necessary, and maintaining open lines of communication?

Why is it necessary to attend to the family of a dementia patient, especially the one with the most responsibility?

Dementia involves a progressive loss of mental capacities and, ultimately, physical and mobility deterioration, leading to a loss of autonomy. Considering this, it is understood that the primary caregiver gradually assumes the functions that the patient is no longer able to perform. All this while also managing self-care, and perhaps the care of other family members (parents, grandchildren...) and coping with a constant emotional process of mourning or adaptation to the losses that occur at each stage.

The role played by the primary caregiver is crucial throughout the course of the disease. They take on everything the patient no longer can do. They are usually the person who ensures the patient follows treatments correctly, in addition to ensuring their safety. Both physically and emotionally, it is a challenging task. That's why dementia impacts not only the patient's life but also the caregiver's life.

- **Find time for yourself***:* Take advantage of respite care to spend time doing something you enjoy. Respite care provides caregivers with a temporary break from constant caregiving, while the person with Alzheimer's continues to receive care in a safe environment. Visit alz.org/care for more information on respite care.

- **Know what community resources are available:** Reach out to the Alzheimer's Association or use our online community resource finder to find services that can help you manage daily tasks.

- **Become an educated caregiver:** As the disease progresses, new caregiving skills may be necessary. The Alzheimer's Association offers programs to help you better understand and cope with the personality changes that often accompany Alzheimer's. Visit the Alzheimer's and Dementia Caregiver Center at alz.org/care for more information and access to caregiving training resources, including free e-learning workshops.

- **Get help and find support:** Seek support from family members, friends, and individuals who can relate to your situation. Take care of yourself. Watch your diet, exercise, and get enough rest. Ensure you stay healthy; this will help you be a better caregiver.

- **Manage your stress level:** Stress can cause physical

problems (blurred vision, stomach upset, high blood pressure) and behavioral changes (irritability, lack of concentration, changes in appetite). Be aware of your symptoms. Use relaxation techniques that work for you and talk to your doctor.

- **Accept changes as they occur:** People with Alzheimer's change, and so do their needs. They may require care beyond what you can provide on your own. Being aware of community resources, from home care services to residential care, should make the transition easier. Support and assistance from those around you will also help.

Finances and Legal Planning

Making decisions about finances and legal planning is crucial to ensure that resources are available and used effectively for the care and well-being of the person with dementia.

Gather Important Documents: In cases of emergency or when the person with dementia can no longer manage their affairs, family members or a legal representative will need access to crucial documents, such as advance directives or financial documents. To ensure that the person with dementia's wishes are fulfilled, keep these documents in a secure place and provide copies to trusted family members or others. An attorney can also retain a copy of these documents.

(Source)

https://www.nia.nih.gov/espanol/planificacion-legal-financiera/planificacion-legal-financiera-personas-demencia

Adaptation to New Dynamics

It is crucial to adapt to new family dynamics as dementia progresses. This may include adjustments to the daily routine, shared activities, and ways of communicating.

Acceptance and Flexibility

Making decisions that foster acceptance and flexibility instead of resisting change is key. Adapting to new circumstances can facilitate the creation of a more positive caregiving environment.

These decisions not only impact the person with dementia but also have a significant effect on the quality of life for the entire family. Collaboration and mutual support are essential for navigating this challenging path.

Acceptance as the Key to Transformation

Acceptance, in the end, became the key that allowed us to enter a new chapter in our relationship with our mother. It was a painful but liberating process. Accepting the new reality allowed us to embrace the woman she was at that moment, with all her vulnerabilities and challenges. It wasn't about giving up the past but finding a way to walk together in the present.

Paths Ahead

Planning and Long-Term Care: Once the truth of the diagnosis settled upon us, we began to explore the paths that opened up. Planning and long-term care became a priority. Anticipating future needs and seeking resources to provide the best possible care for our mother became our shared mission.

Here are some reasons why this is of great importance:

Quality of Care

Long-term planning allows for the establishment of strategies to provide continuous and quality care, addressing the changing needs of the person with dementia as the disease progresses.

Patient Wellbeing

Anticipatory planning can improve the overall wellbeing of the patient by ensuring that decisions are made in line with their wishes and values. This includes choices about care options and respecting their personal preferences.

Relief for the Family

Planning helps alleviate stress and emotional burden for the family by providing clear guidance on how to address caregiving challenges. This may include decisions about where care will be provided and how legal and financial matters will be handled.

Financial Resources

Dementia often involves significant costs, whether in terms of home care, medical services, or specialized facilities. Long-term financial planning allows for an assessment of available resources and informed decision-making about their use.

Legal Planning

This addresses important legal issues such as powers of attorney, living wills, and the designation of healthcare and financial proxies. These documents are essential to ensure that the patient's wishes are respected, and decisions are made in their best interest.

Gradual Transitions

Planning allows for gradual transitions as dementia advances. This may include adjustments to the home environment, the implementation of additional supports, and preparation for changes in medical needs.

Access to Resources

It facilitates access to community resources and support

services, such as caregiver support groups, day programs for people with dementia, and respite services.

In general, planning and long-term care provide a framework that helps effectively address the challenges of dementia, allowing both the affected person and their loved ones to maintain the quality of life as much as possible.

Open Communication: Challenges and Connections

Crucial decisions required open and honest communication among family members. By sharing thoughts and concerns, we realized that each carried their emotional baggage. Despite the challenges, this communication brought us together beyond differences and strengthened our unity.

Open and sincere communication among family members is essential when facing challenges related to dementia. Here are some key reasons why this communication is fundamental:

Shared Understanding

Dementia can affect each family member uniquely. Open communication facilitates shared understanding of the situation, allowing everyone to be on the same page regarding symptoms, disease progress, and changing needs.

Joint Decision-Making

Many decisions related to dementia, such as treatment options, long-term planning, and daily care, require family involvement and consensus. Open communication facilitates joint decision-making, considering the opinions and preferences of all involved.

Emotional Support

Dementia can have a significant emotional impact on family members. Open communication creates a space to express emotions, concerns, and emotional needs, fostering mutual support and understanding during difficult times.

Avoiding Misunderstandings

Lack of communication can lead to misunderstandings and conflicts within the family. Dementia often creates complex situations that require clear understanding and a collaborative approach to avoid unnecessary tensions.

At first, everyone in the family was determined to overcome any communication barriers to prevent misunderstandings and ensure everything flowed smoothly with strength and determination. Over time, everything changed. They let me alone make all the important decisions related to our mother, and that should not have happened. You cannot imagine the high price you have to pay for allowing this.

Advance Planning

Open communication facilitates advance planning. Discussing topics such as care preferences, legal and financial decisions, and the patient's wishes allows for more effective and less stressful planning for everyone.

Division of Responsibilities

In the context of care, open communication helps evenly distribute responsibilities among family members and other caregivers involved. This avoids overburdening a single individual and ensures more effective care.

Fostering Empathy

Dementia can generate frustration and stress. Open communication fosters empathy by allowing family members to better understand each other's experiences and challenges, thereby strengthening family bonds.

In summary, open and sincere communication creates an environment where family members can collaboratively address the challenges of dementia, offering mutual support and making informed decisions for the well-being of all.

Respect for Our Mother's Preferences

An Act of Love

Every decision was guided by the desire to honor our mother's preferences and wishes. Always strong and independent, she deserved to have her wishes respected even in the changing light of her reality. As we discussed options, we tried to ensure that her voice and values were heard within reason.

It was not an easy task, as she demanded her independence as she did before. She wanted to handle her money without any of us intervening; however, this was impossible, as it was dangerous to leave money in her hands. There were losses that we never knew how they could happen.

I made sure she signed a power of attorney for me to handle her finances and that her money was safe and used for her needs.

As we assumed decisions and responsibilities, our roles evolved. From children to caregivers, this should be a shared task, turning us from siblings to advocates and finding strength in family relationships so that everything flows properly. Learn to adapt and support each other while facing storms and sunshine together.

Walking Together, Overcoming Obstacles

The crucial decisions we faced as a family were not without obstacles. From choosing the best medical care to managing daily challenges, each step of the way presented trials that required resilience and empathy. However, we faced these obstacles with a shared sense at the beginning; later, all the responsibility for caring for my mother fell on me. The important thing is that everyone in the family gets involved in every process and medical decisions, all the time. It is a steep path full of ups and downs, and it should not solely fall on a single family member.

Do your best to ensure that your loved one has all the help possible from the family, involve them, make them participate. You are not the savior of anyone; you are providing support and love to that person who needs and deserves to be cared for in this crucial stage. Help them reasonably have a meaningful life, but you must understand that you alone cannot. If your family is not there or does not want to be, still, I suggest you seek support from other entities, even from your community.

In this chapter, we explored how the diagnosis not only brought the truth of dementia but also decisions that shaped our path as a family. Through acceptance, planning, communication, and respect, we learned the importance of coming together as a family to successfully undertake the challenging task of caring for a loved one with dementia.

Chapter 5

My Decision to Take Care of My Mother, the Intense Struggle

After talking to my husband about the possibility of bringing Mom to live with us, I continued to contemplate and pray about it. It wasn't an easy decision; I had to consider the big picture and everything that would be involved. This included making some modifications to the house, quitting my job to fully dedicate myself to her care. I was also taking care of my 6-year-old grandson who suffers from autism. It was necessary to sit down and plan thoroughly, with a clear mind, letting reason be stronger than the heart.

For which of you, desiring to build a tower, does not first sit down and count the cost, whether he has enough to complete it? (Luke 14:28)

Echoes of Love in Dementia

(a poem dedicated to my mother)

On the canvas of memory, subtle dances unfold,

shadows that glide in fragile hallways, stories untold.

The echo of forgetfulness whispers in the gloom,

where yesterday fades, and light dives into the misty room.

In the garden of my mother's memory, flowers wane,

petals falling as time hushes, a muted refrain.

Entangled paths in the tapestry of thought,

where dreams dance in an eternal thought.

The sighs of yesterday intertwine with the mist,

in the corner of forgetfulness, where the mind subsists.

In every gaze of my mother, glimpses of a blurred universe,

where love is understood in its beautiful verse.

Amidst the shadows of dementia, a thread persists,

the bond of affection that time never resists.

HUGGING THE UNCERTAINTY

In the dance of memories, the connection endures,

an eternal bond, in the heart, a faithful lure.

Thus, in the dance of forgetfulness and tenderness,

a poem of enduring love is woven, no less.

Where dementia doesn't extinguish the light of a tie,

and in every note of forgetfulness, my mother's love

is in a warm embrace nearby.

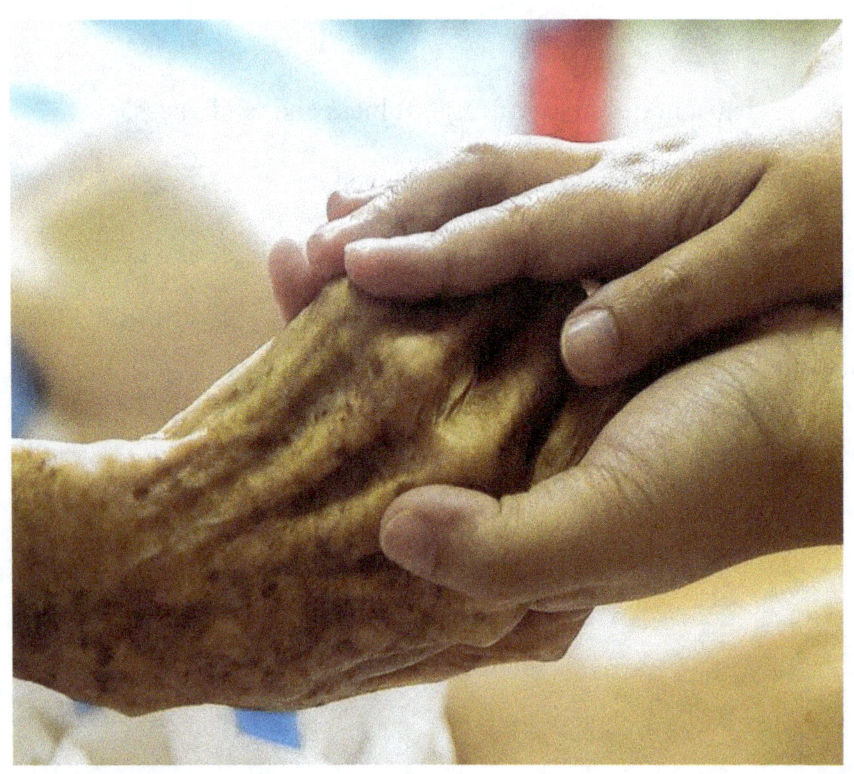

Embracing a Paved Path of Care

The apostle Paul wrote to Christians: "Let them [children or grandchildren] first learn to show godly devotion to their own household and to make repayment to their parents and grandparents, for this is acceptable in God's sight." (1 Timothy 5:4) Elder children offer this "repayment" by acknowledging the years of love, work, and care their parents and grandparents have devoted to them. One way to do this is by recognizing that, like everyone else, the elderly need to be loved and comforted, especially if they are suffering from an illness that requires the loving care and patience of their children. Like all of us, they need to feel valued. They need to feel that their life is worthwhile.

The decision to care for our aging parents is a commitment that arises from deep love and a desire to provide unwavering support in this stage of their lives. For me, there was no hesitation when I decided that I would be the one to take care of my mother. However, what seemed like a clear and simple path turned into a challenge that would test my patience, strength, and love.

The Source of Determination

My mother has always been my example of resilience, the rock upon which I built my strength not to give up in the face of life's challenges. Taking care of her was a natural extension of love and gratitude for all her intense struggles to raise five children. I thought it would be a task I would embrace with ease, as the love I felt for her was a force guiding my decisions. I wanted this process to be as painless as possible for her, as a tribute to her hard work and dedication that she had given us throughout her life.

The Word of God advises: "You should rise up before the gray-haired and show consideration for the elderly." (Leviticus 19:32)

The Reality of Transformation

However, I couldn't help but stumble upon the reality that the mother I knew was no longer the same. Although her strong and determined character still peeked through the shadows, there were new elements in her personality, subtle nuances reflecting the influence of dementia. It was a delicate balance between the past and the present, between the woman she had been and the one being shaped by circumstances beyond her control.

Sometimes, what makes it difficult to honor older parents is the strained relationship children had with them in the past. Perhaps our father was cold and unaffectionate, and our mother, dominant and stern. We may still feel frustrated, upset, or hurt because they were not the parents we wished for. Can these feelings be overcome?

In both family and life situations, this biblical advice is applicable: "Clothe yourselves with the tender affections of compassion, kindness, humility, mildness, and patience. Continue putting up with one another and forgiving one another freely even if anyone has a cause for complaint against another. Just as Jehovah freely forgave you, you must also do the same." (Colossians 3:12, 13)

Taking care of a sick parent is challenging, involving many tasks, responsibilities, and a lot of time. But the hardest part is often emotional. It's distressing to see parents lose health, memory, and independence.

Sandy, from Puerto Rico, shares: "My mother was the core of our family. It was very painful to take care of her when she was so independent. She got progressively worse, needed constant attention day and night. We bathed her, fed her, and read to her. It was very difficult, especially emotionally. When I realized that Mom was dying, I cried because I loved her so much. God's love embraced us and comforted us in a very special way.

The Challenge of Cooperation

Finding ways to collaborate on health matters became a formidable challenge. While she initially cooperated with medical care, over time, even seemingly simple tasks became complicated. The act of taking medications, something that seemed trivial in the past, turned into a struggle between her resistance and my persistence. Every dose, every day, became an emotional and mental battle.

Cooperation in medical care is crucial to ensure that the person with dementia receives proper care. However, as the disease progresses, this cooperation can become an emotional and mental obstacle for caregivers. This chapter explores the difficulties that arise when trying to achieve the cooperation of the person with dementia in health and well-being matters.

Cooperation in medication management can be a significant challenge for both the person with dementia and their caregiver. Here are some common challenges in this aspect:

Forgetfulness and Confusion: People with dementia may experience forgetfulness and confusion, making it difficult to remember the need to take medications regularly. Additionally, they may forget whether they have already taken the dose, leading to situations of duplication or missed medication.

Resistance to Dependency: Some people with dementia resist the idea of depending on others for care, including medication administration. This can manifest as open resistance, refusal of medication, or even hiding pills.

Distrust in Medication: Dementia often affects comprehension. The person may develop distrust toward medications, believing they are harmful or unnecessary. This can make it difficult to persuade them to take the medication.

Changes in Taste and Smell: Some medications may have

an unpleasant taste or aroma. People with dementia may become more sensitive to these aspects, resulting in a refusal to take the medication.

In individuals with Alzheimer's, changes in taste and smell can also affect their appetite and food preferences. Some possible reasons include:

Loss of Olfactory and Gustatory Sensitivity: The disease can affect sensory receptors, making it difficult for the person to perceive tastes and smells as clearly as before.

Difficulties in Recognizing Foods: The person may struggle to recognize foods, influencing their willingness to try new dishes.

Changes in Texture and Temperature: Preferences for certain food textures or temperatures may emerge.

Influence of Medications: Some medications can affect taste and smell as a side effect.

Adapting meals to changing preferences and ensuring proper nutrition is essential. Experimenting with different textures and food presentations, as well as seeking guidance from healthcare professionals, can help address these challenges.

Motor Difficulties: Dementia can also affect fine motor skills, making it difficult for the person to handle pills, open containers, or take liquid medications.

Communication Challenges: Effective communication about the need to take medications can be complicated. People with dementia may have difficulty understanding instructions or expressing if they experience side effects.

Changes in Routine: Disruptions in the daily routine can affect consistency in medication intake. Unexpected events or changes in the environment can cause interruptions in proper administration.

To address these challenges, caregivers can consider strategies such as:

Simplification of the Regimen: Reducing the complexity of the medication regimen can make administration easier.

Use of Visual Reminders: Using calendars, alarms, or visual reminders to help the person remember when to take medication.

Involvement in the Process: Allowing the person to participate as much as possible by providing choices or explaining the need for medication in an understandable way.

Adaptations in Presentation Form: Seeking more pleasant medication formulations, such as liquids or crushable tablets, can facilitate administration.

Establishing Consistent Routines: Maintaining a consistent daily routine can help establish habits in medication intake.

Understanding these challenges and implementing personalized strategies can improve cooperation in medication management and contribute to the overall well-being of the individual.

Daily Battles for Medication

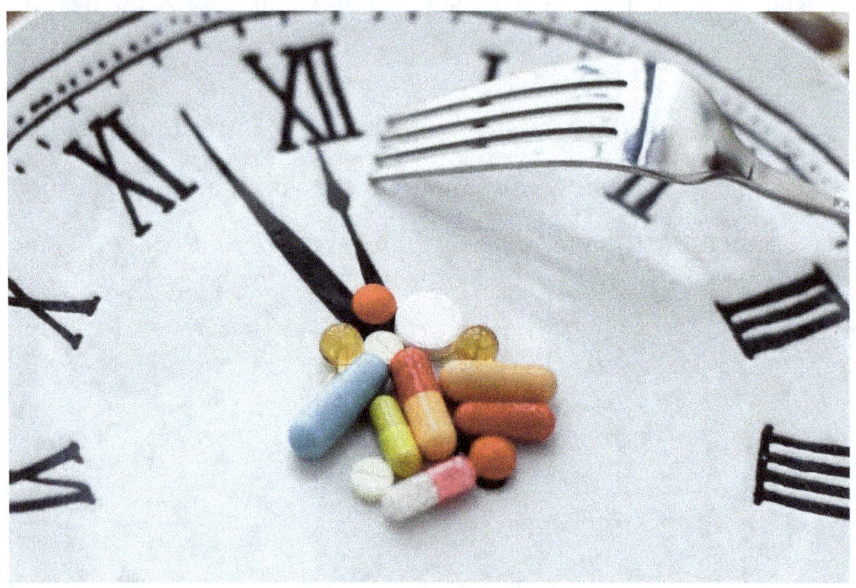

Claudia shares: "As my mother's caregiver, it has been quite a challenge to ensure that she takes her medications according to medical instructions. I discovered that she was pretending to take her pills, hiding them under her tongue and then going to the bathroom to spit them out. The worst part is that many times I didn't notice, as she would flush them down the toilet, making them disappear. There were days when I noticed she was more anxious, confused, and argumentative for any reason. That was the warning sign that led me to pay attention to what was happening. Unfortunately, I had to install cameras even in the bathroom to understand what was happening during her long stays there..."

In the early stages of dementia, the person with the disease may be willing to take their medication without issues. However, as dementia progresses, each medication dose becomes a test of patience and perseverance. The seemingly simple act of taking a pill turns into a constant emotional and mental struggle.

Loss of Perspective

One of the most significant challenges in cooperation is the loss of perspective experienced by the person with dementia. They may forget the importance of medications, refuse to take them due to mistrust, or simply forget that they should. This can cause frustration and concern for caregivers as they seek ways to constantly remind the person of the medication's importance.

"My frustration was evident in not being able to get my mother to take her medication. At first, I opted for strategies that tried to scare her, like saying 'if you don't take your medication, you can die' or 'if you don't take the medication soon, you won't know who I am.' However, my mother clung to her beliefs about medications, arguing, 'You and the doctors want to kill me.' Instead of getting her to take the medications, these words only provoked more anger and resistance from her."

Strategies to Encourage Cooperation

Despite the obstacles, there are effective strategies to

encourage cooperation in healthcare. We will explore how to create medication routines, use visual reminders, and establish a calm and relaxing environment for medication administration. Additionally, we will consider the importance of communication and empathy in addressing this challenge.

Encouraging the cooperation of a person with dementia to take their medications can be a challenge, but there are strategies that might help:

Establishing Routines: Administer medications at specific times of the day and create a consistent routine. Consistency can help the person feel more secure and comfortable with the process.

Using Visual Reminders: Employ visual reminders, such as calendars or boards, to indicate when it's time to take medications. This can help compensate for difficulties with memory.

Offering Choices: Where possible, provide limited choices to give the person a greater sense of control. For example, ask if they prefer to take the medication with water or juice.

Use of Pill Organizers or Automatic Dispensers: Use pill organizers marked with the days of the week or use automatic dispensers to organize doses. This can make the task seem more manageable.

Incorporating Pleasurable Activities: Combine taking

medications with something enjoyable. It could be listening to favorite music, watching a TV show, or receiving a small reward after taking medications.

Involving in the Task: If possible, involve the person in the process. For example, allowing them to hold the glass of water or giving them an active role can make them feel more included.

Speaking Calmly: Maintain calm and patient communication when addressing medication intake. Avoid an authoritarian tone, as this can lead to resistance.

Choosing the Right Moment: Try to administer medications when the person is more relaxed and receptive. Avoid stressful situations that may increase resistance.

Considering Alternative Forms: Consult with the doctor about possible alternative forms of administering medications, such as liquids or patches, if taking pills proves challenging.

Clear Communication: Clearly explain why it's important to take medications and how they can benefit the person. Sometimes, understanding the reason behind the medication can increase cooperation.

Empathetic Communication: Listen carefully to their concerns and fears, and speak with understanding and empathy to establish a foundation of trust.

Simplifying Instructions: Ensure that instructions are clear and simple. Avoid using medical jargon and provide step-by-step information.

Positive Reinforcement: Acknowledge and praise when they cooperate in their care. It may be helpful to use a rewards system or keep a record of achievements to motivate cooperation.

Involving a Mental Health Professional: In some cases, it may be beneficial to consult with a mental health professional with experience in dealing with patients who may resist medical care.

Continuous Education: Provide information about the importance of following medical recommendations and the impact on their health. Sometimes, understanding the consequences can motivate cooperation.

Keeping a Record: Keeping a record of symptoms, medical appointments, and medications can help track progress and facilitate communication with the doctor.

Group Support: It's not a bad idea to join a caregiver or patient support group that can provide guidance and helpful advice on how to address difficult situations.

Be Patient: Patience is crucial. Understand that resistance may be part of the illness and that it may take time to establish strong cooperation.

Remember that each person is unique, so you may need to adapt these strategies according to the specific needs and preferences of the person you are caring for. Open communication and a focus on the person's well-being are fundamental.

The Caregiver's Role in Cooperation

The caregiver plays a crucial role in promoting cooperation. As we navigate the challenge of cooperation in dementia care, let's remember that patience and understanding are key. Each day may present challenges, but with effective strategies and adequate support, we can overcome these barriers and ensure that our loved ones receive the care they need.

Supervision and Reminder: The caregiver can provide constant supervision and reminders to ensure that the person takes their medications as prescribed.

Adaptation to Changing Preferences: Given possible variations in the patient's preferences and behaviors, the caregiver can adapt the way medications are administered to make it more acceptable.

Empathetic Communication: The caregiver's empathetic communication is essential for understanding and addressing any concerns or fears the person may have about medications.

Managing Side Effects: If the person experiences side effects, the caregiver can communicate with the doctor to adjust the medication or explore other options.

Promoting Routines: Establishing consistent routines can help integrate medication intake into daily life, making cooperation easier.

Monitoring Responses: The caregiver can be attentive to the patient's responses to medication and communicate any changes to the medical team.

In summary, the caregiver plays a crucial role in facilitating the patient's cooperation in managing their medications, contributing to overall well-being.

The Desire to Preserve Dignity

As a caregiver, my constant desire has been to preserve my mother's dignity amidst this struggle. I have learned to recognize that her resistance is not merely stubbornness but an expression of her humanity and evolving emotions. As we explore this new territory together, my role is not only to care for her physical needs but also to support her emotional well-being.

It's crucial for caregivers to understand that the resistance of a person with dementia is not simply stubbornness. It's an expression of their evolving emotions. As dementia affects their ability to understand and communicate, resistance becomes their way of expressing desires and needs. In this chapter, we will learn to recognize and understand resistance rather than interpreting it as disobedience.

Emotional Care

People with dementia often experience changes in their

emotional responses. They may have less control over their feelings and how to express them. For example, someone may react excessively to things, have rapid mood changes, or feel irritable. They may also appear unusually distant or uninterested in things.

These changes can be challenging for caregivers. It may be helpful to remember that these changes are partly caused by damage to the person's brain. Someone may react more emotionally to a situation than expected due to a decrease in their ability to think clearly or the loss of objective memories.

It's essential to look beyond the words or behaviors you see, towards the feelings the person might be trying to express. Strong emotions can also be caused by unmet needs. Caregivers should try to determine what these needs are:

Offer the person plenty of praise and encouragement: celebrate successes and focus on positive aspects.

- Avoid harsh criticism or derogatory comments.
- Ensure people have time to engage in activities they enjoy or find purposeful.
- If a person makes a mistake, try to provide as much support as possible.
- Help people maintain existing social relationships and form new ones. This can be done by organizing joint activities

with friends and family, joining hobby groups, and encouraging conversation.

Promoting Autonomy

Despite the progressive loss of autonomy, it's important to encourage independence as much as possible. This chapter will highlight how providing choices and making joint decisions can help preserve the dignity of the person with dementia. From choosing clothing to participating in activities, the caregiver should encourage decision-making.

Here are some tips that may be helpful:

Adapt the Environment: Make adjustments to the environment to make it more accessible and safe. Label objects, use contrasting colors, and eliminate potential obstacles.

Simplify Tasks: Break down daily tasks into simpler steps and provide clear instructions. This makes it easier for the person to do things on their own as much as possible.

Offer Choices: Provide limited choices so that the person can make decisions. This gives them a sense of control and autonomy.

Use Assistive Technology: Consider using devices or technologies designed to support independence, such as voice reminders or monitoring systems.

Encourage Participation: Involve the person in activities tailored to their abilities. It could be folding laundry or participating in recreational activities they find enjoyable.

In my case, increasing the activities that my mother enjoyed helped tremendously and kept her relaxed for long periods of time, such as playing dominoes, bingo, taking walks around a park or lake, watching her favorite TV shows, coloring, and listening to her favorite music. Additionally, I didn't oppose if she wanted to wash the dishes.

Mobility Support: Provide mobility aids such as canes or walkers so that the person can move safely and maintain a certain degree of independence.

"My mother's doctor recommended that even before my mother needed a walker, I should provide it to her so that she could get used to it. People with dementia gradually lose their abilities, and it's challenging to learn a new technique. So, it's a good idea to make their lives easier before they lose all capability."

Establishing Routines: Maintaining predictable routines can provide a sense of structure and help the person perform tasks more independently.

- Try to maintain a consistent routine, such as bathing, dressing, and eating at the same time every day.
- Help the person make lists of things to do, and note appointments and activities in a notebook or calendar.
- Plan activities that the person enjoys and try to do them at the same time every day.
- Consider using a system or reminders to help the person take medication regularly.
- When dressing or bathing, allow the person to do everything they can for themselves.
- Provide the person with loose and comfortable clothing that is easy to wear, such as garments with elastic waistbands,

fabric bras, or large zipper or button pulls instead of laces, buttons, or buckles.

- Use a sturdy shower chair to support an unstable person and prevent falls. You can buy such chairs at a pharmacy or medical supply store.

- Be kind and respectful. Inform the person about what you are going to do step by step while helping them bathe or dress.

- Serve meals in a familiar and consistent place, and give the person enough time to eat.

Social Support: Facilitate social interaction. Connecting with friends, family, or other caregivers can be a source of support and stimulation.

In my case, establishing a routine of taking my mother to church two days a week worked very well. She felt comfortable with the people who attended, and everyone was kind and respectful to her. In fact, many of them called her "the mother of our congregation," which was very gratifying for me. Interacting with spiritual people who understood the important role I was playing as a Christian was rewarding. The elders (pastors in my congregation) prayed with me. I don't remember the specific words they said, but I do remember how I felt. It was as if Jehovah was telling me, 'You are not alone' (Isaiah 41:10, 13). (Visit JW.ORG)

Promoting Self-Care: Encourage the person to engage in self-care activities, such as dressing or grooming, according to their abilities.

Adapting Nutrition: Provide easily manageable and adapted foods based on the person's capabilities. Consider utensils designed to facilitate eating.

Clear Communication: Use clear and positive communication. Ensure that the person understands the information and offer the necessary time to respond.

Preserve Emotionally Important Objects: It is advisable to eliminate superfluous decorative items but keep those that may be emotionally significant and support the person's orientation and identity. These can include family photos or personal mementos.

Celebrate Achievements: Recognize and celebrate achievements, no matter how small. This reinforces self-esteem and motivates the person to continue participating.

Each person is unique, so it is essential to adapt these strategies to individual needs and capacities. Additionally, maintaining a patient and understanding attitude is crucial for supporting the independence of those living with dementia. (You can find more tips on caring for relatives with Alzheimer's at blog.fpmaragall.org)

Celebrating Humanity

As we progress on this caregiving journey, let's remember that our work goes beyond providing care. It's an opportunity to celebrate the humanity of the person with dementia or Alzheimer's. In this chapter, we honor their experiences, emotions, and desires as we work together to preserve their dignity in the dementia journey.

The Daily Renewal of Determination

Every day becomes a renewal of my determination. Sometimes, the path is steep and rugged, filled with obstacles that test my patience and resilience. But amid these struggles, I also find moments of connection—moments when her gaze lights up with recognition or her words reveal glimpses of the woman she once was. It's these small victories that propel me forward.

In this chapter, we explore how the determination to care for my mother has intertwined with the intense struggle of facing the transformation of dementia. As we learn to navigate the turbulent waters of cooperation and resistance, we discover the depth of our love and the importance of finding a balance between physical care and respect for her dignity. Every day serves as a reminder that the caregiving path is a rocky trail of challenges and rewards, and my determination remains a guiding flame through the shadows.

Chapter 6
The Challenges of the Caregiver and Their Care

"Navigating the Waves of Caring Compassion"

The caregiver's role is an act of love that demands unwavering dedication, but it is also a journey fraught with a series of emotional, physical, and mental challenges. In this chapter, we will delve into the challenges that caregivers encounter while taking care of a loved one with dementia, and how self-care also becomes an essential piece of the puzzle.

Three Ways to Prevent Caregiver Stress and Burnout (Daily Caring)

Winner of the 2023 Best Senior Care Website Award

It's one thing to say that you should set aside stress and not dwell too much on things. Another matter is putting this into practice, especially when caregiving extends for years, and concerns are right in front of you.

3 Practical Suggestions:

Have realistic expectations

It's impossible to eliminate all stress, but you can minimize its impact on you. Don't let the fact that you feel stressed cause even more stress! The only caregiver who exists, well-rested, relaxed, and on top of everything, will be found sitting between a unicorn and the abominable snowman (ha!).

Take micro-breaks

Any moment you can release that stress burden will be helpful, even if it's just for 5 minutes. If that means taking an extra 2 minutes in the bathroom to visualize yourself on a beautiful beach or deep breathing, then do it.

Here are a few more ways to take effective micro-breaks:

- Add moments of gratitude to your day.
- Relax in 2 minutes with a helpful (free) mobile app.

- Get 10 quick break ideas for use anytime.

- Get support.

You need and deserve true breaks regularly. It may seem impossible to get help with caregiving, but it's possible to form a team based on the resources available to you.

Realistic ways to take regular breaks from caregiving:

- Explore various ways to get help.

- Hire a few hours of home help each week.

- Leverage local organizations and volunteer resources.

- Find local respite care services.

Recommended for you:

- How to cope with compassion fatigue:

- 8 tips for caregivers

- Five ways to use a journal to reduce caregiver stress

- 5 expert tips to reduce caregiver guilt

- Tips and help for caregivers (DailyCaring.com)

The Weight of Commitment

The commitment to care for a loved one is a choice that carries significant weight. As the caregiver takes on the responsibility of daily needs and the challenges presented by dementia, they often encounter an emotional burden that can be overwhelming. The internal struggle between duty and exhaustion can become a constant challenge.

The internal struggle between duty and exhaustion can be a constant challenge for the caregiver. Often, when we take on the responsibility of caring for a loved one with dementia, we feel a deep sense of duty toward that person. We want to provide them with the best possible care, ensure their safety and well-being, and do everything in our power to improve their quality of life. This sense of duty is a powerful driving force that propels us to face countless challenges and obstacles on the caregiving journey.

However, this sense of duty sometimes clashes with the emotional exhaustion we experience as caregivers. Caring for a person with dementia can be mentally draining. We often face not only the physical fatigue from daily caregiving tasks such as assisting with hygiene, feeding, and mobility but also mental exhaustion. We find ourselves immersed in a world full of uncertainty, mood swings, memory lapses, and constant challenges in communication. The emotional overload can be overwhelming.

Moreover, the feeling of exhaustion is not always related to physical fatigue; it's more of an emotional fatigue. Constantly adapting to the changing needs of the person with dementia, dealing with disagreements that may arise, and feeling like we no longer have time for ourselves can push us to the limit.

This clash between duty and exhaustion is often exacerbated by the profound transformation of the relationship between the caregiver and the person with dementia. The person we are caring for, who was once a source of support and guidance, now depends entirely on us. The relationship is often reversed, and we find ourselves caring for someone who in the past may have been an independent and self-sufficient parent, spouse, or relative. Accepting this role reversal can be painful and emotionally exhausting.

When Love Turns into Obligation

The commitment to care for a loved one is a journey marked by the intensity of love and responsibility. As the caregiver embraces this task, they find themselves holding a significant weight that transcends physical and emotional dimensions. Dementia adds a complex nuance to this commitment, presenting challenges that can make the burden overwhelming.

Gabriel confesses that caring for his father with Alzheimer's made him experience anticipatory grief, as he saw his father gradually change, stating: "It felt like I had already lost my father even before he passed away."

Anticipatory grief is an emotional process experienced by many individuals caring for a loved one with a progressive illness such as dementia, where they feel as if they have already lost the person before their actual passing.

This experience is common among caregivers due to various factors:

Loss of the person they once knew: Dementia transforms the personality and identity of the affected person. Caregivers often miss the relationship they used to have with their loved one before the illness.

Changes in the relationship: The disease can lead to significant changes in the relationship between the caregiver and the person with dementia. This may include the shift from a role of a loved one to a caregiver role, which can be emotionally challenging.

Difficulty in communication: Communication becomes more challenging as the disease progresses. Caregivers may feel that they cannot connect or communicate in the same way with their loved one.

Preparation for loss: As dementia advances, caregivers often know that they will eventually lose their loved one. This can create a sense of anticipatory grief and anticipation of the impending loss.

Anticipatory grief can be an overwhelming and painful experience for caregivers. It can manifest in a wide range of emotions, such as sadness, anxiety, frustration, anger, and sometimes even relief. Facing and processing these emotions is an important part of self-care for caregivers.

It is crucial to seek emotional support through support groups, therapy, or talking to friends and family who can understand the situation. Accepting the reality of the disease and trying to find moments of connection and meaning in the relationship with the person with dementia can also help manage anticipatory grief.

Unwavering Responsibility

The responsibility of caring for a loved one with dementia is not just a choice; it becomes a calling that resonates deeply in the caregiver's heart. The commitment is woven with threads of love but also with the understanding that taking on this role involves unwavering dedication. The struggle to provide care and support becomes an act of profound devotion.

The Reality of Duty

As dementia unfolds in everyday life, the caregiver finds themselves holding a duty that cannot be taken lightly. The duty to meet daily needs, from administering medication to performing basic tasks, becomes a constant responsibility. The weight of these tasks can lead to exhaustion and emotional pressure.

According to the National Center for Biotechnology Information, caregivers are four times more likely to develop depression and three times more likely to seek treatment for anxiety compared to non-caregivers. In addition, the Family Caregiver Alliance reported that various chronic conditions, such as heart diseases or crises, cancer, diabetes, and arthritis, prevail almost twice as much in caregivers than in non-caregivers.

If you still hesitate to seek assistance from external resources, I suggest starting by asking people close to you for help with easy and specific tasks. For example, you can ask them to cook a meal, pick up a prescription, or spend a short time with the person you care for. Some people will tell you how much they can help. It may not be easy, but the right people who are willing and able will provide support. If it becomes a necessity, consider options such as home care or adult day care centers. It may be challenging to envision someone else providing help, but you should consider whether your circumstances and ability to provide care are most appropriate in the long run.

The Emotional Challenge

The commitment to caring for a loved one with dementia also entails a profound emotional challenge. Mood fluctuations, memory loss, and communication difficulties can impact the caregiver's emotional stability. The feeling of constant adaptation can give rise to emotions of confusion, sadness, and even frustration and anger.

The caregiver's anger toward the person with Alzheimer's is a complex phenomenon that can arise due to emotional burden, constant stress, and challenges associated with caring for someone with dementia.

Some reasons that could contribute to this anger include:

Frustration with Communication: Dementia can affect communication, making the person with Alzheimer's less understandable or cooperative. This frustration can lead to anger.

Difficulties in Personal Care: Assisting with daily tasks such as bathing or feeding can be challenging and exhausting, generating feelings of anger.

Here are some tips that can help:

Practice Empathy: Try to understand the feelings and perspectives of the person you are caring for. Empathy can help manage anger by recognizing both parties' emotions.

Take Breaks: Schedule regular breaks to avoid burnout. Fatigue can increase frustration and anger, so taking care of yourself is crucial.

-"My mother always went to bed early, no later than 7:00 pm. Once she was asleep, my relaxation ritual began. I filled my bathtub with hot water, added bubbles, lit scented candles, played classical music in the background, and, of course, a glass of exquisite red wine couldn't be missing. I stayed there for a reasonable amount of time, in complete tranquility."

Establish Routines: Predictable routines can make tasks more manageable. Consistency can reduce resistance and stress associated with daily activities.

Clear Communication: Explain tasks clearly and simply. Use calm and positive language to minimize resistance and frustration.

Something that worked for me when I couldn't get my

mother to bathe when I wanted was to take a shower first and put on a fragrance she liked. When she saw this, her mind perhaps connected the bath and the fragrance with going for a walk. Immediately, she would ask me to bathe her and apply fragrance. Both of us would relax, and afterward, as a reward, we would go for a coffee to her favorite café.

Offer Limited Options: Where possible, provide limited choices to make the person feel more in control. For example, ask if they prefer to wear a certain color of clothing. In my case, I would choose two blouses with two colors my mother liked... Mother, which one do you prefer, purple or green? This way, she felt acknowledged, and I didn't lose control of the situation.

Seek Professional Help: If you feel it's challenging for you to manage anger, don't hesitate to consult with health professionals or occupational therapists for specific advice on caregiving techniques and anger management.

Incorporate Enjoyable Elements: Combine tasks with pleasurable activities whenever possible. For example, listen to music during bath time or share a special meal.

Adapt the Environment: Make adjustments to the environment to make it safer and more comfortable. This may include grab bars, non-slip pads, or adapted utensils.

Learn Relaxation Techniques: Both for yourself and the

person you are caring for, learning relaxation techniques can help manage stress and reduce anger. I suggest the 4-7-8 relaxation technique. Inhale through your nose, pulling with your diaphragm to fill your lungs with air in 4 seconds. Hold the air for 7 seconds, and then exhale through your mouth in 8 seconds as gently as you can. Repeat this exercise 10 to 15 times.

Seek Support: Connect with other caregivers in similar situations. Sharing experiences and advice can provide valuable emotional support.

Remember that caregiving can be exhausting, and it's normal to feel a variety of emotions, including anger. Seeking help and using practical strategies can make these tasks more manageable for everyone.

Change in Relationship: Dementia can alter family dynamics and change the relationship between the caregiver and the affected person. This can lead to resentment and anger.

Adjustment to New Roles: The change in roles, where the caregiver takes on more responsibilities and the person with dementia becomes more dependent, can create tensions and anger.

Financial and Logistical Difficulties: Caring for a person with dementia can involve financial and logistical challenges. These additional concerns can contribute to caregiver anger.

Seek Professional Help: Consulting with mental health professionals can provide additional tools for managing stress and anger healthily.

It is important to remember that experiencing anger does not mean a lack of love or care. It is a human response to a challenging and stressful situation.

If you regularly experience signs of stress, consult your doctor. Ignoring these symptoms can deteriorate your physical and mental health.

(Alzheimer's Association)

The Internal Struggle: Duty vs. Exhaustion

The internal struggle between the duty to care and the accumulating exhaustion often becomes a difficult dilemma to resolve. Love and devotion sometimes clash with the reality of fatigue and emotional overload. The caregiver may feel trapped between the need to provide care and the recognition of their own limitations.

The Challenge of Balancing Changing Roles

The transformation of the relationship with the loved one can be overwhelming. Transitioning from a filial role to a caregiver role can create internal tensions. Love and duty toward the loved one often compete with the need to take care of oneself. Balancing being a caregiver and preserving one's mental and emotional health becomes a delicate act of self-discipline and self-love.

Margaret's experience highlights the emotional weight she faced when taking on the care of her aunt with Alzheimer's. Despite emotions affected by the end of her marriage, she chose this monumental task. Initially, she thought it would be manageable, given the shared love and connection through shared solitude. However, as her aunt lost her mental faculties, the emotional burden became overwhelming. In moments of exhaustion, she was forced to briefly step away to deal with her own emotions, even if it caused anxiety in her aunt. Lack of privacy exacerbated the situation, illustrating the emotional and physical challenges faced by caregivers in similar situations.

My Own Care Path

In my life, the experience of taking care of my mother has become a monumental journey. My heart feels torn between a deep sense of duty and the emotional exhaustion that often overwhelms me. This exhaustion is not just physical; it is a mental burden that accumulates day after day. I find myself trying to balance my own needs with the devotion I feel towards her.

Taking care of someone with dementia is a task that requires a lot of time and energy. Often, caregivers experience discouragement, guilt, abandonment, sadness, frustration, confusion, or anger; all of this is completely normal. The responsibility can feel like a burden in various ways. Therefore, it is important to give yourself time and space to reaffirm that you are doing your best even when it may not seem like it. Try to reconsider the words you direct to yourself in a different way. For example, you can practice repeating some of these phrases internally:

- I am doing the best I can.
- It's the illness speaking.
- What I'm doing would be challenging for anyone.
- I am not perfect, and that's okay.
- I cannot control some things that happen; only how I react to them.
- Even when I do everything possible to help, the person with dementia will still have symptoms and complications because of the illness, not because of what I do.
- I will cherish the moments of peace we can have together.

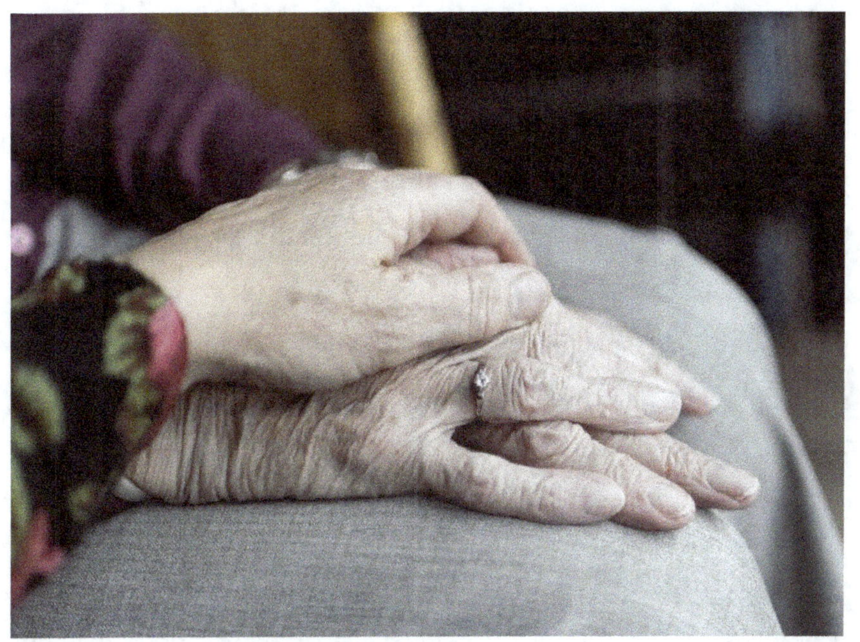

The Satisfaction of Your Spiritual Needs

Since you are caring for someone with dementia, you may need more spiritual resources than others. Mental health experts have noted that many caregivers benefit from fulfilling their spiritual needs as it helps them cope with difficult moments and provides a sense of calm and balance. This may not be suitable for everyone, but if you are part of a faith community, make sure to take some time to connect with it. For others, the best way to find inner peace and meet spiritual needs may simply involve focusing on meditative practices or believing in a God, the creator of all things, capable of hearing the prayers of those going through overwhelming and painful situations such as caring for a loved one with dementia.

In His Word, the Bible, Jehovah God lovingly provides very beneficial advice for those taking care of their elderly parents, though that is not the only help He offers. "Jehovah is near to all those calling on him," wrote the inspired psalmist, "...he will hear their cry for help, and he will save them." Jehovah will save, meaning protect, His faithful even in the most difficult situations. (Psalm 145:18, 19.)

Confronting the Changing Reality

At times, I confront the harsh reality that the role my mother played in my life has taken a turn. She, who was once my guide and support, now depends on me in a way I never would have imagined.

Accepting this reversal of roles is painful and involves the internal struggle of admitting that my mother, the independent and self-sufficient woman I knew, now needs my constant help.

Myrna, from the Philippines, experienced this when caring for her mother with Alzheimer's. "There is nothing more depressing than seeing a loved one suffer and not being able to tell you where it hurts," writes Myrna. "It was like watching her gradually drown in her mind without me being able to do anything. Many times, I would kneel down and tell Jehovah how tired I felt. I cried like David when he pleaded with Jehovah to put his tears in a skin bottle and remember him. [Psalm 56:8.] And Jehovah supplied the strength I needed according to His promise. 'Jehovah became a support to me.' (Psalm 18:18.)

From Caregiver to Protector

In my quest to find balance between duty and exhaustion, I have learned to embrace my role as a protector of my mother. My sense of duty often clashes with my own overwhelming emotions. The tears I shed are not just for myself but for her and the life we both face together. My emotional fatigue is a sign that I am investing my heart in her care.

Facing Daily Struggles and Demands

The daily fights and arguments are a constant reminder of the complexities of dementia. My mother, in her confusion and frustration, often expresses her emotions in a way that challenges my patience. My role as a caregiver extends beyond physical tasks; it involves being an emotional refuge, even though at times, I feel I can barely take care of myself.

Challenge of Reconciling Lost Independence

One of my greatest challenges is reconciling the independence my mother has lost with the brave woman still residing within her. Accepting her vulnerability leads me to confront my own vulnerability, and sometimes I plunge into denial. Despite internal struggles, I continue to learn that self-compassion is crucial on this journey.

A Necessary Balance and the Search for Self-Empowerment

As I navigate this internal struggle, I strive to find a necessary balance. My love and sense of duty continue to guide me, but I also recognize the importance of taking care of myself. Finding moments of relief and support is essential to prevent total exhaustion. This internal struggle challenges me to empower myself and make decisions in the best interest of both my mother and myself.

My daily struggle with caring for my mother and family matters finally took its toll. I realized I'm not Wonder Woman, that chronic stress had taken control, and my exhaustion overshadowed reason. In that forest ablaze with unaddressed emotions, where everything turned gray from the smoke, I got lost. The light was no longer visible, and I plunged into a terrifying scene. It was then that I remembered the words of the Psychoanalyst Dr. César Silvas and his comparison with emotional smoke that prevents you from seeing the whole scene clearly.

I decided to take action and seek help to emerge from that dense darkness. Psychological therapy became my salvation, a true blessing in my life. Now, little by little, things are making sense again, and my ability to reason has resurfaced. Accepting that I needed support to lighten the burden was a crucial step towards peace. Therapy has become my beacon in the midst of this challenging journey, illuminating the path as I regain clarity and emotional balance.

It can be overwhelming to think about the high costs associated with psychological therapy, so many people going through uncontrolled situations, where emotions cloud reason, and mental health is at risk, decide not to seek help. There are many free or very low-cost programs on social media and online platforms that can greatly assist you in giving proper attention to your mental health.

Here is a list of them:

Mejor Hablemos: In Mejor Hablemos, you will find psychologists with extensive training and experience, guaranteeing you the best service. They offer a personalized approach to understand and work on your problems or concerns.

Instituto Mexicano del Seguro Social (IMSS): IMSS also provides a Telephonic Medical Guidance in Mental Health service through the number 800-2222-668, option 4, where psychologists and psychiatrists provide assistance, from Monday to Friday from 08:00 to 20:00 hours.

Universities: University hospitals often have programs that provide patients with access to interns and residents on a sliding scale payment system, which is usually much less expensive than that of private mental health providers. We recommend contacting hospitals in your area to inquire if they have any of these programs.

Local Mental Health Centers and Clinics: There are numerous associations and organizations that focus on providing mental health services at affordable prices or helping people whose economic means do not allow them to access such services. The governmental site MentalHealth.gov maintains a list of such associations that we recommend checking to find the best option for your case.

Support Groups: Mental health is not only addressed through personal therapies and medications. Another excellent option that many people find useful is support groups. Support groups are spaces where people going through similar situations can come together to share their stories and experiences in a way that helps reduce isolation and loneliness.

Low-Cost or Free Independent Psychologists: Many psychological offices calculate their fees based on a sliding scale. This is simply a way to calculate the cost of therapy through variable fees based on a person's income. Both non-profit clinics and private practice therapists use this method at times to make therapy accessible to people who cannot afford their standard fees. In return, they get the satisfaction of supporting individuals who otherwise could not pay for their services and increase their client base.

Medicaid: By law, all Medicaid plans provide access to mental health services. However, the scope of these programs varies from state to state, so we recommend reviewing your plan to understand the services it covers. Some of the services that may be included are counseling, therapy, medication management, social work services, peer assistance, and substance abuse treatment. (Information based on saberespoder.com)

The Internal Struggle as an Opportunity for Growth

Despite the internal struggle between duty and exhaustion, this battle can also be an opportunity for personal growth. As the caregiver faces challenges and finds ways to cope with emotional overload, they can develop skills of self-compassion, patience, and resilience. This struggle can lead to a deeper understanding of oneself and greater empathy toward others.

Seeking Support and Personal Care

Recognizing the internal struggle and its effects is a crucial first step. The caregiver must prioritize self-care and seek support. By setting healthy boundaries, asking for help, and allowing moments of rest, the caregiver can find a healthier balance between duty and exhaustion. Support from other caregivers and healthcare professionals can be invaluable in this process.

Facing Guilt and Self-Compassion

The internal struggle often comes with feelings of guilt. The caregiver may feel guilty for needing a break or for experiencing contradictory emotions. Practicing self-compassion and acknowledging that taking care of oneself is not selfish but necessary can help mitigate this guilt. Self-compassion allows the caregiver to be kind to themselves while continuing to provide support.

Rediscovering the Meaning of Care

As the caregiver confronts the internal struggle and seeks balance, they may rediscover the true meaning of care. Care goes beyond daily tasks; it involves being present, listening, and providing emotional support. Finding ways to balance duty and exhaustion can lead to a more authentic and meaningful relationship with the loved one.

The Search for Balance

Amidst this weight, the caregiver embarks on a constant search for balance. Finding ways to meet the demands of care without sacrificing one's own well-being is a challenge that requires creativity and resilience. Balance is a fine line that is redefined as the situation evolves.

Recognizing Humanity in the Commitment

It is important for the caregiver to recognize their own humanity in the midst of this commitment. Imperfection is part of the journey, and acknowledging the need for rest, support, and self-care is not a sign of weakness but of wisdom. Strength lies not only in the act of caring but also in the ability to take care of oneself.

Strength in Committed Love

Despite the challenges and the weight that sometimes seems overwhelming, the caregiver's committed love shines as a source of strength. As the caregiver faces each day with determination and compassion, the depth of their commitment is demonstrated. Every act of care, no matter how small, becomes a reminder of the profound connection between the caregiver and the loved one.

Balancing Demands

Caring for a loved one often coexists with the demands of daily life. Working, taking care of the family, maintaining a functional home—all of this adds to the equation. Finding a balance between caring for the loved one and self-care can be a challenging task, especially when each day presents a new set of obstacles and changing needs.

The Battle of Exhaustion

Physical and emotional exhaustion is a reality that many caregivers face. Sleepless nights, constant demands, and emotional weight can quickly deplete a caregiver's resources. The line between caring for others and caring for oneself can become blurred, and exhaustion can erode the caregiver's physical and mental health.

Loss of Personal Identity

As the caregiver immerses themselves in the role of providing care, they may sometimes lose sight of their own identity. Personal needs and desires can take a backseat as the caregiver focuses on the well-being of their loved one. This loss of identity can lead to feelings of isolation and disconnection from the outside world.

Emotional Rollercoaster

The caregiver often faces an emotional rollercoaster. From sadness at witnessing their loved one change to frustration over daily challenges and joy in moments of connection and clarity, emotions can swing drastically. The caregiver may feel as if they are caught in a whirlwind of intense feelings.

"There were moments when great sadness welled up in my chest as I watched my mother, gazing out the window into the backyard with a secretive expression, as if searching for answers to unasked questions. I immersed myself in her world, trying to decipher what was going through her mind in those moments. However, everything changed when I saw her coloring her flower books, an activity that brought her unparalleled satisfaction.

Her illuminated gaze and childlike smile, full of contentment as she precisely colored those beautiful flowers, filled me with joy and tranquility. However, every night, as I lay down, unanswered questions would arise in my mind: Did I do well? Was I unfair in scolding her for not wanting to eat the carefully prepared dish? Am I a selfish daughter for thinking that maybe she would be better off in a nursing care facility? These unanswered questions echoed in my head, tinged with conflicting feelings, triggering tears that flowed for hours. And upon waking up the next day, the same secretive dynamic would restart once again."

Caring for the Caregiver: A Crucial Priority

Amidst the challenges of caring for a loved one with dementia, the caregiver's personal care must not be overlooked. Caring for the caregiver becomes a crucial priority to maintain physical and mental health. Self-care, time to rest, and seeking emotional support are essential to prevent exhaustion and stay upright during this journey.

Edna D. Santiago, author of the book "Para cuidar… hay que cuidarse" (To care... you have to take care), describes very important personal factors that generate stress in the caregiver:

- The relationship with the person affected by Alzheimer's, the sense of emotional loss, and adjustments to move forward as a caregiver.

- Emotions felt when witnessing a loved one deteriorate and being unable to stop the disease.

- Acceptance of the disease in the person being cared for.

- The demands of effort involved in caring for a person with cognitive problems and erratic behavior.

- The time spent as a caregiver, fatigue, and tiredness resulting from long hours spent providing care.

- The loneliness and social isolation experienced by the caregiver.

- Loss of independence and freedom to control their time to do what they enjoy.

Financial complications.

- Family conflicts and lack of support.

- Lack of appreciation from family members for the care provided to the person with Alzheimer's.

- Sleep problems or interrupted sleep due to the person being cared for.

The Journey of Self-Care: From Division to Changing Reality.

At first, when my siblings and I reached an agreement on who would take care of my mother, I willingly accepted the responsibility. We thought that dividing the tasks would make the burden more manageable for me. Initially, this division served as an effective strategy to address my mother's care. She spent some days with my siblings, giving me a break.

Changes in Comfort and Emerging Anxiety

However, as time progressed, changes in the caregiving dynamics began to emerge. Stepping out of her comfort zone became a challenge for my mother. She experienced anxiety in unfamiliar environments. She stopped visiting my siblings and sought refuge in my home, where she felt safe. My house, once a place of shared comfort, has now become her constant sanctuary.

The balance became even more delicate as demands multiplied. My role as a caregiver intertwines with the expectations of a husband who also requires attention and time. Juggling between these responsibilities becomes an exercise in emotional and temporal juggling. Finding time for myself becomes an even greater challenge.

Part of self-care includes the challenge of educating others about the nature of dementia. Explaining how this disease affects daily life and changes in family dynamics has become exhausting. Often, people do not understand the true depth of what I am facing. The disconnect between my experience and others' understanding creates a sense of isolation.

Questioning the Legitimacy of Emotions

I find myself questioning whether it is okay to complain about the physical and mental work involved in caring for my mother. Sometimes, I feel guilty for expressing my exhaustion and frustration. Society may convey the idea that caregiving is an unbreakable duty, leading to questioning whether it is allowed to feel overwhelmed or angry.

"It is frustrating when, expressing concerns about caring for my mother, I received responses that minimized my feelings. Attention often focused on the role of being a daughter and the supposed obligation, sidelining my emotional well-being. Some people express phrases like 'it's your duty as a Christian to take care of her' or 'you should be grateful to have your mother' or 'be thankful for taking care of her' 'what I wouldn't give to be able to take care of my mother' 'thank God you still have her...' However, rarely did I hear questions about how I was or if I needed support.

I longed to hear, 'How are you? Are you being compassionate to yourself? Is there anything I can do for you? Take the day off; I'll take care of her so you can rest or do whatever you want to do; if you have medical appointments to attend to, I'll take care of her so you can go without any worry. This time, I'll take our mother to that medical appointment to give you a break...'" I longed for more people to show compassion, offer practical help, and acknowledge the emotional burden that comes with caring for a loved one with dementia.

I am grateful to God for all the help given by one or two people who genuinely cared about me. The lack of understanding from my siblings and the scant empathy from some close ones made this journey even more challenging.

In Search of Answers in Self-Care

My path to self-care involves seeking answers and solutions to face this challenging reality. I am exploring ways to receive help, delegate tasks, and find resources that alleviate the burden. I understand that self-care is not selfish; it is an act of preserving my well-being to continue providing the best possible care for my mother.

Seeking Support and Strength

The caregiver should not face these challenges alone. Seeking support from other caregivers, support groups, and healthcare professionals can be a source of strength. Sharing experiences and advice can alleviate the sense of isolation and provide valuable perspectives for facing daily challenges.

Seek support from others. You are not alone—many others are caring for someone with dementia. Locate the nearest Area Agency on Aging, the local chapter of the Alzheimer's Association, a California Caregiver Resource Center, or visit the Family Care Navigator (www.caregiver.org/family-care-navigator) to find support groups, organizations, and services that can assist you. Anticipate that, like the loved one you are caring for, you will have good and bad days. Develop strategies to ease the bad days.

In this chapter, we explore the challenges the caregiver faces while navigating the path of caring for a loved one with dementia. From the weight of commitment to emotional exhaustion and the struggle for balance, each challenge is an opportunity for growth and learning. At the same time, we highlight the importance of the caregiver's personal care as a way to maintain the strength and resilience necessary to face this journey with compassion and love.

Chapter 7

Embracing Uncertainty

"Experiences of individuals who have confronted the painful disease of dementia in their loved ones."

Maria and her mother: Maria shared her experience of caring for her mother, who suffered from advanced Alzheimer's. As the disease progressed, her mother stopped recognizing her and often became aggressive towards her and her sister. Maria described the sadness of witnessing her mother lose her independence and personality.

Our family, in its everyday dynamics, suffered an abrupt interruption like the eruption of a volcano. Even though mom still had moments of clarity, she longed for her car, her independence, and the freedom to do as she pleased. She fiercely fought while she had the strength to maintain her autonomy.

Nights turned into endless vigils when mom demanded to return to her home. During those dark hours, she wandered through the house, turning on lights, disturbing the children's sleep, and plunging us into a world of cries and screams. Sometimes, her aggression would unleash, and she would attack us with hits or bites. What was even more painful, our beloved matriarch began uttering hurtful and cruel words, words we had never heard from her lips.

Every evening became a torment in helping her with the most basic tasks, from eating to bathing or brushing her teeth. Some nights, my sister and I were forced to sleep by her side to protect her during her incessant awakenings. But even in those moments of care and protection, we couldn't escape the overwhelming weight of the nightmare we lived through every day.

This is the chronicle of our journey through dementia, an emotional eruption that tested our family in ways we never imagined. In the midst of the storm, we sought answers, support, and, above all, a way to stay united in love and compassion as we faced the relentless challenges of mom's illness.

Juan and his grandfather: Juan cared for his grandfather for several years as dementia progressed. Despite the challenges, Juan shared how he found moments of connection through music, as his grandfather used to be a passionate pianist.

Juan, a dedicated caregiver, faced years of challenges while taking care of his grandfather amid the relentless progression of dementia. However, in the midst of the darkness of this disease, Juan discovered a beautiful source of connection: music.

His grandfather, in his youth, had been a passionate pianist. Music flowed through his fingers and filled his home with melodies of joy and nostalgia. But as dementia took hold of his mind, his ability to play the piano slowly faded.

Juan, with love and patience, decided to use music as a bridge to his grandfather. Even though words faded into the dementia fog, musical notes were a universal language that both could understand. He dusted off the piano in the house and started playing his grandfather's favorite songs.

As the melodies filled the room, something magical happened. His grandfather's tired eyes lit up with recognition, and his hands, which used to dance on the keys, came back to life, if only for a brief moment. Together, they shared a journey through the notes, exploring songs that had been the soul of his grandfather.

These moments of connection through music became a beacon of light in the midst of the dementia storm. Juan and his grandfather shared laughter and tears as music reminded them of who they were and how love could transcend even the boundaries of memory.

This is the story of how Juan found beauty and comfort amid

dementia, through the melodies that connected his heart with his grandfather's.

Linda and her husband: Linda recounted her experience caring for her husband diagnosed with early-onset Alzheimer's. As her husband lost his cognitive abilities, she became his primary support. Linda emphasized the importance of finding support groups and resources for caregivers in similar situations.

Linda's story is a testament to the love and dedication that one can show while caring for a loved one facing early-onset Alzheimer's. As her husband battled this disease, Linda became his rock, his unwavering support amid the fog of dementia.

Early-onset Alzheimer's slowly took away her husband's cognitive abilities. Words became elusive, memories faded, and everyday tasks became overwhelming challenges. Linda, with courage and love, took on the role of the primary caregiver. But she didn't do it alone.

Linda understood the importance of seeking help and support. She joined local and online support groups, where she could connect with other caregivers facing similar challenges. Here, she found a safe space to share her concerns, joys, and frustrations. Together, they shared strategies and advice for dealing with dementia.

The process was overwhelming. Linda went through nights

of insomnia, moments of frustration, and tears of helplessness. But she also experienced moments of deep connection with her husband. Even though words often got lost in the Alzheimer's fog, the love they shared was unbreakable. In moments of lucidity, they held onto the beauty of their relationship.

Throughout their journey, Linda and her husband sought valuable resources. They participated in occupational therapies and activities that stimulated the mind. Linda became a tireless researcher, seeking the latest research and therapies that could help her husband.

This is the story of how Linda and her husband faced early-onset Alzheimer's together, supporting each other in the midst of the storm. Through love and a constant search for support and resources, they found the strength to deal with this debilitating disease. Their story is a reminder that love can shine even in the darkness of dementia.

Carlos and his father: Carlos shared how Alzheimer's disease drastically changed his relationship with his father. They went from being close friends to a caregiver and son role. Carlos expressed how, despite the challenges, he learned to find moments of joy in his interactions with his father.

Carlos's story is a poignant account of how Alzheimer's disease can profoundly transform a family relationship. He shared how he went from being a close friend and a loving son to becoming the primary caregiver for his father as they faced the challenges of this relentless disease together.

Carlos described how Alzheimer's drastically changed his father's personality and behavior. The man who was once a pillar of strength and wisdom now struggled with memory loss, confusion, and dependence. For Carlos, this change was heartbreaking.

As he took on the caregiver role, Carlos found himself facing a series of emotional and practical challenges. He had to learn to deal with his father's mood swings, waves of confusion, and occasions when his father didn't recognize him. It was a journey filled with sadness and despair, but there were also moments of profound joy.

Carlos shared how, amidst the storm of the disease, he learned to find those moments of joy and connection with his father. He discovered that music was a bridge to communicate when words failed. Together, they listened to songs his father used to enjoy, and they sang together. In those moments, Alzheimer's seemed to recede, at least for a while.

Despite the challenges, Carlos found the strength to carry on. He surrounded himself with support, including caregiver groups and friends who understood his situation. He learned to take care of himself while caring for his father and discovered the importance of compassion and patience.

This is the story of how Carlos and his father faced Alzheimer's together, weaving new memories amid adversity. Their story is a reminder that, even in the most challenging circumstances, love and connection can endure, offering moments of light in the midst of darkness.

Ana and her aunt: Ana recounted how her aunt developed dementia and became her primary caregiver. As the disease progressed, her aunt experienced episodes of confusion and paranoia. Ana spoke about the importance of patience and compassion in caring for her loved one.

Ana's story is a touching testimony of how the bond between a niece and her aunt strengthened as they faced the challenges of dementia together. Ana shared how she became her aunt's primary caregiver when she developed the disease and how that experience changed their lives in profound ways.

Ana described how dementia affected her aunt, causing episodes of confusion and paranoia. The woman who had once been strong and self-assured now struggled with memory loss and an inability to recognize those around her. It was a painful and bewildering time for both of them.

As dementia advanced, Ana found herself taking on an increasingly active role as a caregiver. She had to learn to deal with her aunt's moments of confusion and distress, which was not always easy. However, Ana emphasized the importance of patience and compassion on this journey.

Ana shared how, despite the challenges, she found ways to connect with her aunt on a deeper level. She learned to adapt to her loved one's changing needs and provide constant emotional support. Patience became her ally, allowing her to remain calm in moments of turmoil.

In the midst of adversity, Ana and her aunt wove a bond based on love and devotion. Despite the dementia that had stolen part of her aunt's identity, Ana continued to care for her with affection and understanding. Their story highlights the importance of maintaining connection with our loved ones despite difficulties, reminding us that love and patience can be guiding lights on the path of dementia.

Nidia and her mother: I have taken on the role of guardian for my mother, being her emotional anchor to provide security. Previously, I was an independent person, about to start my own cleaning business. However, my mother's dementia changed the course of my life. Although she is calm, the burden of caring for her constantly overwhelms me, affecting my emotional well-being.

We live at home with 9 more people, including my grandchildren. My mind is on alert all the time, restructuring my mother's life with patience and affection, but guilt sometimes takes over when, at the end of the day, due to being busy with other household matters, I don't give her the attention she deserves. I miss the mother who used to advise me wisely, the one who comforted me in my sad moments. She was my safe place.

Although I am not her only daughter, the necessary help to take care of my mother and attend to her needs is scarce. Not everyone has the courage and determination for this arduous task; all the responsibility falls on my shoulders. I love my mother with all my heart, and I undoubtedly want her to live her last days with much love, but I must recognize the need to reclaim my own life; it is vital to find my lost identity.

"It is normal for those caring for a loved one with a chronic illness to feel disheartened," says the publication "Caring for the Person With Dementia."

"As the disease progresses, the loss of a companion and a cherished relationship is keenly felt. It is disheartening to think about how things were before."

Jennifer explains her family's feelings as they witnessed her mother's health deteriorating: "We were grieving. We missed her lively conversation. We felt very sorrowful."

Gillian adds, "I didn't want my mother to die, and I didn't want her to suffer either. I cried a lot."

It has been said that caring for elderly parents is a "story without a happy ending." Despite all efforts, parents eventually pass away, as has been the case for many who have shared their stories here. But those who trust in Jehovah know that death is not the end of the story. The apostle Paul said, "I have hope toward God [...] that there is going to be a resurrection of both the righteous and the unrighteous." (Acts 24:15.) Those who have lost their elderly parents are comforted by the hope of resurrection and the divine promise of a wonderful new world, where "death will be no more." (Revelation 21:4.)

Chapter 8

Weaving a Support Network

How Friends, Neighbors, and the Community Can Ease the Caregiver's Burden"

"The person responsible for a sick individual may wonder, 'Why did this have to happen to me? Why am I not receiving help from anyone? Don't they realize I can't handle it all? Couldn't the patient be more cooperative?' Sometimes, the apparent unfair and increasing demands of the patient and other family members may be very irritating.

In the previous chapters, we discussed the importance of taking time for yourself away from the responsibilities of caring for a dementia patient and dedicating it to your own well-being. In this chapter, we will address the types of support that would make this feasible and can come from family, friends, or neighbors.

Perhaps you need someone to stay with the patient part of the day, or maybe a place where your relative could stay for a few days while you take a break or receive medical attention. It would be advisable for the person you are caring for to be in a place where they are well taken care of by other people, either with acquaintances or a care facility where they can be safe away from you. This kind of support is called 'Respite,' as it allows you to take a break from the patient's care for a while.

The caregiver's role for a person with dementia is a monumental task, full of emotional and physical challenges. In previous chapters, we have explored the complexities of this journey and the importance of self-care. Now, let's focus on an invaluable source of support: the community surrounding the caregiver. In this chapter, we will explore how friends, neighbors, and the community at large can contribute to easing the caregiver's burden by providing time, emotional support, and respite opportunities.

The Power of Community

Loneliness and isolation are common struggles for caregivers. In this section, we will discuss how involving friends and neighbors in the caregiving process can create a vital support system. We will share inspiring stories of caregivers who have relied on their networks of friends and neighbors and how this has improved their quality of life.

Building a Support Team

How can you communicate your needs to friends and neighbors? We will explore effective strategies for establishing strong connections and how to talk about what you really need. Additionally, we will discuss the importance of setting clear boundaries and expectations in these support relationships.

When seeking support from friends and neighbors in your caregiver role, it is essential to build strong connections and communicate your needs effectively. Here, we will explore how to build a solid support team and how to openly and honestly talk about what you really need. We will also highlight the importance of setting clear boundaries and expectations in these support relationships."

1. Open and Sincere Communication:

Open and sincere communication is the foundation of any supportive relationship. Talk to your friends and neighbors about the demands and challenges you face as a caregiver. Be honest about your emotional and physical needs. Vulnerability in these conversations can foster a deeper understanding.

2. Educate about Dementia:

Often, friends and neighbors may not fully understand dementia and its implications. Provide educational information about the disease and its impact on your loved one. This can help create a solid knowledge base in your support community.

You can organize informative meetings where you share details about dementia, its challenges, and how they can help. Providing educational materials, such as brochures or reliable websites, can also be helpful. Additionally, encourage them to participate in support groups for a deeper understanding and to offer more effective support.

3. Make a Clear List of Tasks and Needs:

Create a detailed list of specific tasks and needs that could be addressed by friends and neighbors. This makes it easier for people to know in which areas they can offer their help and alleviates uncertainty. Develop a list of the medications the person you are caring for takes, the schedule, and the dosage. This will help those providing assistance keep track of them throughout the day and serve as a reminder.

4. Establish Limits and Expectations:

Talking about your limits and expectations is essential. Make it clear when you need help, what type of help is acceptable, and when you prefer to do things on your own. Establishing these limits is vital to avoid frustration or misunderstandings.

5. Encourage Continuous Communication:

Encourage your friends and neighbors to communicate with you regularly about your situation. Sometimes, people might hesitate to offer help, thinking they are interfering. Keep communication lines open so that people feel comfortable sharing their intentions to support you.

6. Explain How They Can Help:

Provide clear suggestions on how your friends and neighbors can assist you. For example, they can offer to do grocery shopping, take care of your loved one for a while, or simply listen when you need to vent. The more specific your requests, the more effective the support will be.

7. Express Thanks and Recognition:

Don't forget to express thanks and recognize the support you receive. Gratitude strengthens relationships and encourages people to continue helping. You can express your thanks in many ways, from a simple word of gratitude to small gestures of appreciation.

8. Maintain an Open and Tolerant Mindset:

Each friend or neighbor can provide support differently. Keep an open and tolerant mind toward their efforts and willingness to help. Not everyone has the same skills or availability, but their support remains valuable.

In summary, building a support team with friends and neighbors involves open and sincere communication, education, clear limits, and well-defined expectations. Through continuous communication and fostering an environment of mutual understanding, you can effectively leverage this valuable source of support in your role as a caregiver.

CHAPTER 9

The Moderate Stage in Alzheimer's And Its Characteristics

The moderate stage in Alzheimer's is an intermediate phase in the progression of the disease, situated between the mild (initial) stage and the severe (advanced) stage. During this stage, symptoms and cognitive decline become more evident and pronounced than in the mild stage, but they have not yet reached the level of total disability experienced in the severe stage.

Common characteristics of the moderate stage of Alzheimer's:

Difficulty with short-term memory: Individuals in this stage may have difficulty remembering recent events and details such as names and dates. In dementia, difficulties with short-term memory manifest as an inability to retain new information for an extended period. People may forget recent conversations, recent events, or even the performance of daily tasks. This loss of immediate memory significantly impacts the ability to function independently in daily situations. It can be frustrating for both the affected person and those caring for them.

Forgetting recent events: Individuals with dementia may have difficulty recalling events that happened recently. This could include recent conversations, meals, or activities performed on the same day.

Temporal disorientation: Temporal disorientation is common in this stage. Individuals may lose track of the day, date, and even the time of day. They may confuse morning with afternoon or the current day with a previous one.

Temporal disorientation in dementia involves difficulty understanding and following time. Affected individuals may lose track of the day, date, time, or even the season. This can lead to situations where the person thinks they are in a different time. For example, they may believe they are in a past period of their life or that certain recent events happened a long time ago. This temporal disorientation can cause confusion and anxiety in the affected person.

Forgetting names and faces: Remembering names and recognizing faces becomes problematic. Individuals may not recognize close family members or friends, causing distress for both them and their loved ones.

Difficulty following conversations: Maintaining a coherent conversation can become a challenge. Individuals may lose the thread of what they are saying or what others are talking about, leading to confusing responses.

Difficulty with daily tasks: Everyday activities that were once simple, such as cooking a meal or getting dressed, can become overwhelming due to the difficulty in remembering the necessary steps.

Dependence on reminders: Individuals with dementia often rely on visual or written reminders to perform simple tasks. Posters, sticky notes, and reminder clocks can be helpful.

Repetition: Repeating questions or stories is common. The person may ask the same question multiple times in a short period due to the inability to remember the answer. Repetition in conversations is common in individuals with dementia, especially in moderate stages. They may repeat the same questions, stories, or comments several times, sometimes in a short period. This may be due to short-term memory loss and difficulty retaining information. To manage this, it's important to be patient, respond kindly, and, if necessary, redirect the conversation to another topic. Establishing routines and providing simple answers can help reduce anxiety associated with repetition.

Frustration and confusion: Difficulty with short-term memory can lead to frustration and confusion for both the person with dementia and their caregivers. It's important to stay calm and provide support during these times. Addressing these emotions with compassion and patience is essential. Offering clear and simple instructions, maintaining a structured environment, and supporting activities that stimulate the mind can help reduce frustration and confusion. Additionally, emotional support and affectionate communication are crucial for providing comfort and understanding emotions amid confusion.

For caregivers and family members, understanding these difficulties in short-term memory is crucial. Providing a structured environment, maintaining consistent routines, and using understandable communication strategies can help individuals with dementia face these challenges more effectively and provide them with a greater sense of security.

Communication problems: Communication becomes more difficult. Individuals may have trouble finding the right words or following a conversation.

People may have difficulty finding the right words, following a conversation, or expressing their thoughts coherently. Language comprehension may also decrease. Adapting to these challenges by being patient, using clear and simple language, and encouraging nonverbal communication, such as gestures and facial expressions, is important. Creating a calm and distraction-free environment can enhance the person's ability to communicate. Additionally, listening empathetically and showing affection contribute to maintaining meaningful connections.

Aphasia: Aphasia is the loss of the ability to comprehend or express words coherently. Individuals with dementia may struggle to find the right words or express their thoughts clearly.

Difficulty following conversations: Following a conversation can become complicated. Individuals with dementia may lose track of what others are saying and may respond inappropriately.

Repetitive speech: Repeating words, phrases, or questions is common. This can be frustrating for caregivers, but it's important to stay calm and respond patiently.

Nonverbal communication: Individuals with dementia often rely more on nonverbal language, such as gestures, facial expressions, and tone of voice, to communicate. Caregivers should pay attention to these signals.

Comprehension problems: Understanding what is being said to them may be limited. They may take words literally or misinterpret information.

Incoherence: Speech can become incoherent and lack sense. Words may be improperly combined, making understanding difficult.

Frustration: Communication difficulties can lead to frustration for both the person with dementia and their caregivers. It's important to maintain a compassionate and patient attitude.

Use of stereotypies: Individuals with dementia sometimes use repetitive or stereotypical language patterns, such as saying the same words or phrases over and over.

These repetitive behaviors may stem from memory loss and difficulty retaining new information. They may also be a way of expressing anxiety, discomfort, or simply a strategy for coping with uncertainty.

In these situations, it's important to remain calm and respond with patience. Providing reassuring answers and distracting with activities or changing the subject can help manage repetition. It's also recommended to establish structured routines to provide a sense of security and predictability.

Loss of reading and writing ability: In advanced stages, individuals may lose the ability to read and write.

Affected individuals may have difficulty understanding written words, remembering letter sequences, or experiencing issues with grammar and coherent writing. This is due to changes in the brain areas associated with language processing and memory.

To support someone with dementia in this situation, it's helpful to simplify written communication, use images or graphics, and focus on alternative forms of expression, such as verbal communication or activities that do not depend on reading and writing. Adapting the environment to minimize dependence on these skills can facilitate engagement and communication.

Mutism: In some individuals, advanced dementia can lead to mutism, meaning they stop speaking altogether.

When a person with dementia stops speaking entirely, it can be an emotional challenge for the caregiver. It's important to explore the possible reasons behind this loss of speech, which may include changes in the brain areas responsible for language, anxiety, frustration, or simply difficulty finding the right words.

To address this situation, some strategies can be attempted:

Create a quiet environment: Reduce noise and confusion in the environment to create a more relaxed space that can foster communication.

Nonverbal communication: Encourage communication through gestures, facial expressions, and eye contact. Sometimes, nonverbal communication can be more effective.

Meaningful activities: Involve the person in activities they used to enjoy, such as listening to music, viewing photos, or engaging in other forms of nonverbal expression.

Consult health professionals: A doctor or a dementia specialist can offer guidance and specific suggestions based on the individual situation.

Provide emotional support: Ensure that the person feels

safe and understood. The loss of speech may be related to emotions that are difficult to express.

Adapting to Changing Needs: As the disease progresses, communication needs may change. Be open to adjusting approaches and seeking new ways of connection.

It is essential to work collaboratively with healthcare professionals and dementia specialists to provide the best possible support to the affected person.

To address these communication issues, it is crucial to use clear and simple language, maintain effective nonverbal communication, and be patient and understanding. It is also important to pay attention to the emotional and physical needs of the person with dementia to better understand their communication attempts.

Spatial and Temporal Disorientation: The person may get lost in familiar places, forget the date or time, and have difficulty recognizing their location.

Individuals with dementia may struggle to recognize familiar places, such as their own home or neighborhood. They may even get lost in familiar places and have trouble understanding the layout of their surroundings. For example, they may not remember where the bathroom is in their own home or how to get to the kitchen.

Loss of the sense of time is common. People with dementia may forget the date, the day of the week, and even the season. They can confuse the past and the present, believing they are living in a previous period of their lives.

Confusion in Recent Events: They may have difficulty remembering recent events, such as what they did that morning or whether they have eaten. This can lead to repetitive behaviors, such as eating multiple times in a row.

Loss of Orientation: As the disease progresses, they may lose the ability to orient themselves in their environment. This can lead to dangerous situations, such as leaving home and getting lost.

Day and Night Confusion: Dementia can also affect the person's circadian rhythm, meaning they may be awake during the night and sleep during the day. The reversal of the sleep cycle, where the person with dementia may be more active at night and drowsy during the day, is common and is known as "irregular sleep-wake syndrome" or "dementia-related sleep-wake syndrome."

Here are some strategies that could help manage day and night confusion:

Establish Consistent Routines: Maintaining regular schedules for daily activities such as eating, bathing, and exercising can help reinforce the circadian rhythm.

Exposure to Natural Light: Exposing the person to natural light during the day, especially in the morning, can help regulate their biological clock.

Limit Caffeine and Stimulation Before Bed: Reduce caffeine intake and avoid stimulating activities before bedtime to facilitate sleep.

Create a Sleep-Conducive Environment: Keep the bedroom dark, quiet, and comfortable. Consider using blackout curtains and other elements to create a sleep-friendly environment.

Avoid Prolonged Naps During the Day: If possible, limit daytime naps to encourage more solid sleep at night.

Consult with Healthcare Professionals: If the reversal of the sleep-wake cycle becomes a significant challenge, it is important to discuss it with the doctor or other healthcare professionals specializing in dementia.

Social Consequences: Spatial and temporal disorientation can lead to social withdrawal, as individuals with dementia may become insecure about where they are and what is happening around them. This can contribute to a sense of isolation.

Stress and Anxiety: Constant disorientation can be stressful and distressing for both the person with dementia and their caregivers.

To deal with spatial and temporal disorientation, caregivers should take steps to ensure a safe and familiar environment. This includes keeping important objects in accessible and consistent places, establishing a predictable daily routine, and providing clear reminders about the time and date. It is also essential to offer emotional support and understanding to the person with dementia when they experience confusion.

Difficulty in Problem-Solving: Problem-solving and decision-making skills are affected.

Changes in Personality and Behavior: Changes in personality, such as irritability, anxiety, apathy, or repetitive behaviors, may arise. These changes can include:

Irritability: The person may become easily upset or frustrated, sometimes without an apparent reason.

Anxiety: They may experience anxiety, feel nervous, or worried.

Apathy: A loss of interest in activities they once enjoyed, coupled with a decrease in motivation.

Repetitive Behaviors: Repeating words, questions, or activities can become a pattern.

Verbal or Physical Aggression: In some cases, the person may become verbally or physically aggressive, which can be a response to confusion or frustration.

Changes in Eating Habits: Changing food preferences or showing disinterest in food may occur.

Changes in Sexuality: Changes in the expression of sexuality, from a loss of interest to inappropriate behaviors, may arise.

These changes can be challenging for both the person with dementia and their caregivers. It is essential to address these behaviors with compassion and understanding. Effective communication, establishing routines, and adapting to changing needs can help manage these challenges. Additionally, seeking support from healthcare professionals and support groups can be beneficial for caregivers.

Difficulty in Performing Daily Tasks: Everyday tasks, such as dressing, bathing, or cooking, become more challenging and require supervision or assistance.

Increased Dependence: The person may become more

dependent on others for basic activities.

Impairment of Motor Skills: Mobility and coordination problems may worsen. This can manifest in various ways:

Unsteady Gait: The person may have difficulty walking securely, with unsteady steps or imbalance.

Coordination Issues: Fine and gross motor coordination may deteriorate, affecting the ability to perform tasks like dressing or eating.

Swallowing Difficulties: Swallowing may become more complicated, increasing the risk of aspiration and feeding problems.

Muscle Stiffness: Muscle stiffness may develop, affecting mobility and flexibility.

Inability to Perform Complex Motor Tasks: Activities that were once routinely done, such as buttoning buttons or using utensils, may become challenging.

These changes can have a significant impact on independence and the quality of life of the person with dementia. It is crucial to adapt the environment to ensure safety and seek guidance from healthcare professionals, such as physiotherapists and occupational therapists, to effectively address these challenges.

Sleep Changes: They may experience disruptions in the sleep pattern, such as insomnia or excessive daytime sleepiness.

Feeding Problems: They may have difficulty eating or drinking properly.

It's important to note that the progression of the disease can vary significantly from person to person, and not everyone will experience the same symptoms or at the same pace. During this stage, ongoing care and support, as well as the adaptation of care strategies, are essential to improve the quality of life for the person with Alzheimer's and reduce the burden on caregivers.

Learn about the most common types of dementia.

Dementia is a generic term used to describe a variety of neurological conditions that affect the brain and worsen over time.

Alzheimer's Disease:

Abnormal protein deposits form amyloid plaques and tau tangles throughout the brain.

It is the most common form of dementia, affecting memory, thinking, and the ability to carry out daily activities.

Vascular Dementia: This form of dementia is caused by problems with blood supply to the brain. It can result from strokes or problems in blood vessels.

Lewy Body Dementia: This disease is characterized by the presence of abnormal protein aggregates in the brain. It can cause fluctuations in cognition and symptoms similar to Parkinson's disease.

Frontotemporal Dementia: Primarily affects areas of the brain responsible for behavior and personality. It may manifest as personality changes, impulsive behaviors, and language difficulties.

Inclusion Body Dementia: Associated with the accumulation of abnormal proteins in brain cells and can affect memory, language, and behavior.

HIV-Related Dementia: Affects some people with HIV and can cause cognitive impairment.

Creutzfeldt-Jakob Disease: A rare condition affecting the central nervous system, leading to rapid changes in personality, uncontrolled movements, and cognitive decline.

Huntington's Disease-Related Dementia: A hereditary disease affecting coordination, behavior, and cognition.

Traumatic Dementia: Occurs as a result of traumatic brain injuries, such as those related to concussions or head injuries.

Mixed Dementia: In some cases, a person may experience more than one type of dementia simultaneously.

Each type of dementia has specific characteristics and may require different care approaches. The diagnosis and proper management of dementia depend on the specific type and the individual's health status. (For more information, visit cdc.gov)

Chapter 10

Children and Adolescents Living with a Person with Dementia, How They Can Understand It

When children and adolescents live with a family member affected by dementia, it is essential to approach the situation in a compassionate and educational manner. Young individuals may experience a range of complex emotions when witnessing changes in their loved ones. Providing information about the disease, encouraging the expression of feelings, and offering emotional support are crucial aspects. Additionally, promoting meaningful activities and moments of connection can help build relationships amidst the challenges presented by dementia.

It is crucial for children to understand what is happening to the confused person and why they act in a certain way for several reasons:

Reducing Fear and Confusion: Understanding dementia and its associated behavior helps reduce the fear and confusion that children or adolescents may experience when witnessing changes in their loved ones. It's easier for them not to get angry with the affected family member when they understand why they do or say certain things. Help them understand that the person is suffering from a disease that destroys part of the brain, making it unable to function normally. This is why they forget names, become clumsy, or cannot speak correctly. Sometimes, children or adolescents may get upset about trivial things the affected person does or says. Help them understand that this is because their brain no longer comprehends what is happening (even if explained to them). The brain structures governing their behavior have also been damaged, so the affected person cannot control their actions or take care of themselves.

Promoting Empathy: Understanding the disease fosters empathy in children, allowing them to see beyond challenging behavior and develop compassion towards the affected person. It is normal for children or adolescents to worry about what will happen to their demented loved one, or perhaps wonder if they can make the situation worse by not understanding what is happening. Help them become more empathetic so they can treat the affected person with respect and cultivate great patience. Even if children sometimes do something that irritates the affected person, assure them that nothing they do can worsen the situation. The affected person may get angry or irritated momentarily because of them, but that does not worsen their disease.

Preparing for Changes: Children may feel more secure and prepared to face the changes brought about by dementia when they understand the course of the disease and its effects. Encourage children or adolescents to learn more about dementia. Provide them with books on the subject and encourage them to ask questions when they feel overwhelmed by the affected person's behavior or when their health is rapidly declining. Many children or adolescents may feel frustrated by the changes they are experiencing when having a family member with dementia at home. They have to adapt to new changes, which can bring anger and frustration. Even in the best circumstances, living with a person affected by a dementia-related condition is difficult.

Here are some experiences of young people who found it very difficult to adapt to the changes:

Daniel, 12 years old: "I have no privacy, my grandmother barges into my room without warning and starts rummaging through my drawers..."

Adriana, 15 years old: "I can't make noise, and I can't play my favorite music at medium-high volume because my grandfather gets upset."

Jonathan, 7 years old: "The way my grandfather eats turns my stomach; I simply retreat to my room if he's in the dining room."

Angel, 16 years old, mentions: "I can't invite my friends over because my grandmother gets upset, and I don't want to bring them because she does things that embarrass me."

Kendra, 10 years old, says: "They took away my room to give it to my grandmother; now I have to share my sister's room."

Carlos, 8 years old: "Everyone is so busy with Grandpa, and they end up so tired that we never do anything fun as a family anymore. I feel rejected."

Alondra, 6 years old: "I'm scared that my grandmother will die."

Robert, 9 years old: "My parents get mad at me more often than before."

Does your child identify with any of these cases? It's possible that most children have some of these concerns or mixed feelings when having a family member with dementia at home due to the changes they are experiencing. It's advisable for adults to sit down and talk with the affected children in this case and work together to find solutions to improve the situation. Some young people have mentioned that the worst problem is not the behavior of the person with dementia but how their parents act.

For practical help and resources for children and adolescents living with a family member with dementia, consider:

Specialized Organizations: Look for organizations dedicated to supporting people with dementia and their families. Many of them offer specific resources for children and adolescents.

Reliable Websites: Explore reliable websites about dementia, such as those from Alzheimer's associations, which often have sections dedicated to family members and caregivers, including children.

Health Professionals: Consult with health professionals, such as psychologists or counselors, who can provide personalized guidance and recommend specific resources for the family situation.

Bookstores and Libraries: Look for children's and youth books about dementia. They can provide educational and comforting perspectives for young people.

Local Support Groups: Participate in local support groups. Sometimes, these groups address the specific needs of children and adolescents, offering an environment to share experiences and obtain resources.

Summary, Acknowledgment, and Conclusion

In the journey through these pages, we have explored the complexities, challenges, and, most importantly, the love that surrounds those facing dementia. Although the words shared here may not encompass the entire experience, I hope they have served as a beacon of understanding and comfort.

Closing this book, I invite every reader to reflect on the strength, patience, and compassion that reside in caregivers and those who share the path with dementia. Beyond the pages, let us remember that each story, each experience, is unique. May this knowledge inspire us to build bridges of understanding and support in our own lives.

May this book serve as a reminder that, even in the darkness of dementia, love and connection can shine brightly. I sincerely appreciate every moment you have dedicated to these shared stories and hope you find solace and wisdom to face the challenges that may come your way.

"I want to express my deep gratitude to all the brave individuals who shared their experiences of living with a family member with dementia. Their narratives have enriched this book with genuine perspectives, offering comfort and wisdom to those facing similar challenges. I sincerely appreciate their generosity in opening their hearts and sharing their stories, contributing to the collective understanding of dementia and providing support to those in need. Thank you for being the guiding light for others on this journey."

To my dear daughter Angie,

I want to express my profound gratitude for being my unwavering support in this challenging journey of caring for my mother with Alzheimer's. Your understanding, patience, and love have been crucial in every step of this journey. Your constant presence and willingness to face challenges together have given me strength and comfort.

Your kindness and dedication have not only lightened my burden but have also illuminated the dark moments with the warmth of your affection. I cannot find enough words to thank you for being my rock and sharing this demanding path with me.

Thank you for being more than a daughter, for being my companion on this journey. Your support has made an invaluable difference, and I am eternally grateful to have you by my side. May Jehovah bless you always!

With love and gratitude,

Almangie Ruefli

References and Resources:

Organizations:

Alzheimer's Association

- Website: https://www.alz.org
- 24/7 Helpline: 800.272.3900

DaylyCaring

- Website: https://www.daylycaring.com
- Tips and assistance for caregivers

Asociación Mexicana de Alzheimer y enfermedades similares

Fundación Alzheimer

- Tel/Fax: 55-23-15-26

National Hospice Organization

- Tel: 703-243-5900

National Mental Health Association

- Tel: 303-762-7922

NIA Alzheimer's and related Dementias Education and Referral (ADEAR) Center

- 800-438-4380
- Email: adear@nia.nih.gov
- Website (English)
- Website (Spanish)

CaringInfo (National Hospice and Palliative Care Organization)

- Tel: 800-658-8898
- Email: caringinfo@nhpco.org
- Website (English)

Centers for Medicare & Medicaid Services

- Tel: 800-633-4227
- TTY: 877-486-2048
- Medicare Website (English)
- Medicare Website (Spanish)

JW.ORG (Official Website of Jehovah's Witnesses)

Provides resources related to faith, the Bible, and daily life from the perspective of this religious community. Offers guidance on applying biblical principles in daily life, including situations such as caring for individuals with chronic illnesses.

Books and References:

- The 36- Hour Day: A Family Guide to Caring for People Who Have Alzheimer's (Nancy L. Mace)

- To Take Care of Loved One... You need Care of Yourself (Enna D. Santiago)

- Learning to Speak Alzheimer's (Joanne Koening Coste)

- Creating Moments of Joy for the Person with Alzheimer's or Dementia. (Jolene Brackey)

- Surviving Alzheimer's: Practical Tips and Soul-Saving Wisdom for Caregivers (Paula Spencer Scott)

- Thoughtful Dementia Care: Understanding the Dementia Experience. (Jennifer Ghent-Fuller)

- Activities to Do with Your Parents who has Alzheimer's-Dementia. (Judith Levy)

About The Author

Almangie Ruefli is a passionate advocate for the well-being of the elderly and a dedicated expert committed to exploring the complexities of dementia and caring for affected loved ones. Her deep connection to the subject is built on a solid foundation of thorough research, interviews with dedicated caregivers, and valuable experience working in nursing homes.

This dedication is reflected not only in her writing but also in her commitment to understanding comprehensively the challenges faced by those caring for people with dementia. Almangie Ruefli shares not only professional knowledge but also personal experiences, including her own journey with her mother affected by dementia.

The combination of her experience in the health field, direct interaction with caregivers, and emotional connection to the subject makes Almangie Ruefli offer a unique and valuable perspective. Her work not only informs but also provides emotional support to those who share the burden of caring for loved ones with dementia.

www.ingramcontent.com/pod-product-compliance
Lightning Source LLC
Chambersburg PA
CBHW071426150726
48000CB00001B/491